RECONSTRUCTION

MACMILLAN AND CO., LIMITED
LONDON · BOMBAY · CALCUTTA · MADRAS
MELBOURNE

THE MACMILLAN COMPANY
NEW YORK · BOSTON · CHICAGO
DALLAS · ATLANTA · SAN FRANCISCO

THE MACMILLAN COMPANY
OF CANADA, LIMITED
TORONTO

RECONSTRUCTION

A PLEA FOR
A NATIONAL POLICY

BY

HAROLD MACMILLAN, M.P.

MACMILLAN AND CO., LIMITED
ST. MARTIN'S STREET, LONDON
1933

First Edition, December 1933.
Reprinted, December 1933.

PRINTED IN GREAT BRITAIN

PREFACE

WHILE this book was being written a revival of business activity was taking place. There has been a considerable increase in our imports of raw materials and our exports of United Kingdom manufactures. The figures of registered unemployed have declined and the number of insured workers in employment has shown a steady increase throughout the whole of 1933.

This evidence of revival is supported by the more thorough index of business activity compiled by the *Economist*, which comprises a series of eighteen component indices, based upon the year 1924.

A study of the whole course of the crisis as it affected Britain reveals a basic strength and resilience which encourages the hope that the improvement of recent months will be continued. The mood of optimism which has been created in business circles as a result of these improvements is also to be welcomed, but this optimism must not be allowed to cloud our judgment and lead to an acceptance of the view that the signs of recovery are a justification of inaction.

There is a sense in which, paradoxical as it may seem, Britain may be in greater danger from recovery than from depression. The lessons of the long period of depression might soon be forgotten if it appeared that we were going to win back to prosperity without further effort on our own behalf. There is always a sufficient readiness to accept any plausible excuse for doing nothing. For to do nothing unusual is the complacent course we would all prefer, especially when there are risks and difficulties to be faced in any action we might adopt.

The proposals advanced in this book have been written, as has been said, during the period in which revival has been taking place. It is submitted that even if the revival should exceed the most optimistic anticipations, some such policy is still essential to recovery and stability.

A quotation from the *Economist* of October 21st dealing with the index of business activity makes a suitable introduction to what must be said regarding the dangers of assuming that our troubles are over.

> "The index (of business activity) touched its highest point between August and November 1929. The decline did not come immediately, for as late as April 1930 the index was within two points of its maximum. From then on, however, the descent was steep and almost continuous. There were some signs of stability in the autumn of 1930, but they proved deceptive, and throughout the winter of 1930–31 the decline was as rapid as ever. In the second quarter of 1931, however, there were clearly marked signs of recovery, and between April and July the index rose by nearly 1 per cent.
>
> ". . . Once again a rising tendency was cut off by events, for in August 1931 the political and financial crisis broke upon the country. For four months the decline was resumed more steeply than before. The depreciation of the pound seemed, however, to have a favourable effect, for the index

touched bottom in November 1931 and recovered so rapidly that by April 1932 more than half of the ground lost since the onset of the crisis had been regained. From April 1932 the pace has been slower, unless the encouraging figures of the last few months are to be taken as marking the beginning of a new trend. For the whole period since the suspension of the gold standard to date the average rate of incline of the curve has been about 4·2 per cent. per annum. This is a gratifying and perhaps surprising result. Excessive self-congratulation should, however, be stilled by the reflection that at this rate of recovery we shall not rejoin the 'projected' trend of 1924–29—itself a disappointment—until some time in 1939. We have reason to be thankful that since the autumn of 1931 we have not suffered any intensification of the crisis; but we have succeeded in doing very little more than hold our own, and very much more rapid progress must be shown before we can talk of real recovery."

The number of insured persons unemployed in September 1933 was 2,375,000, or 18 per cent. of the insured population. The percentage unemployed in the principal industries was as follows:—

Coal-mining	32·8
Building, Public Works, etc.	26·4
Engineering, etc.	22·7
Transport	20
Cotton	22·3
Wool	10
Shipbuilding and Repairs	54·1
Iron and Steel	29·4

Distributive Trades . . .	11·8
All other Industries . . .	14·4

In discussing the trend of business activity the years 1924 and 1929 are regarded in retrospect as the "boom" years of the post-war period. The fact should never be lost sight of, however, that in 1929, which was the most prosperous year in the last decade, there was an average of about 1,200,000 insured persons unemployed. The *Economist* index holds out some hope that, if nothing occurs to interrupt the process, we may again reach the 1929 level of prosperity in 1939—that is, in four or five years' time. But even so there is every reason to suppose that the same level of business activity will mean a much greater volume of unemployment than that which confronted us in 1929.

All the indices would seem to support the view that Britain has been suffering from a depression which arises out of the basic disequilibrium in world production to which we have only begun to adjust ourselves in a haphazard way, following upon the introduction of Protection. Upon this basic crisis, arising from the ill-adjusted balance of national production, the financial crisis of 1931, which plunged us into a deeper depression, was superimposed. We are recovering from the worst effects of the second blow to our stability. The balancing of our budget; the suspension of War debt payments; the abandonment of the gold standard which tied our currency to an exchange level we could not support, have all contributed to the measure of recovery we now enjoy. But there is still left with us the problem which has confronted the nation ever since the War. Until this problem is solved and unemployment completely overcome, both by the extension of work and the extension of leisure, there can be no slackening of the effort for which energy has been engendered by the depths of depression and the seriousness of our situation in recent years.

H. M.

London, November 1933.

CONTENTS

CHAPTER I

THE NEED FOR A POLICY

If we can assume that Britain will escape the catastrophe of war or civil disturbance, then it is probable that when the history of the present period comes to be written, it will be seen as a hiatus between the old economic system and the new. It is a period which cannot yet be dignified by the name transition. For to visualise a transition it is necessary to see more or less clearly both the beginning and the end of the process. The history of events has made us familiar with the framework of the system which we are leaving behind. Unfortunately there is no such clarity about our destination. Nor is social inventiveness even keeping pace with the pressure of events. The great need of the moment is not only for a policy of action to deal with a pressing situation, but for a new theory of social and economic organisation which will facilitate the evolution towards a new economic system suitable to the changed circumstances of the modern world.

If, on the other hand, war or civil disturbance intervenes, the present will be seen in retrospect as a period in which the helpless futility of moderate men prepared the ground for catastrophe, and their lethargy or incompetence created the situation in which the violent and ruthless could appeal successfully to the passions of a disillusioned and despairing people. Revolutionary movements can only grow with the development of a revolutionary situation. So it was in eighteenth-century France; so it has proved in modern Russia, Italy, and Germany. The revolutionary situation, however, can only develop as a result of the bankruptcy of statesmanship and the impoverishment and discontent consequent upon a deepening or protracted economic crisis.

In Britain we have still time to think. Let us face the fact frankly, however, that we have time only because of the buffers which have wisely been created between the worker and destitution. The cushion of social services on which he is able to fall in times of depression may not be so soft as more prosperous people imagine; but it has served the purpose in recent years of at least assuring a basic minimum of subsistence, while efforts to induce recovery were carried out. Nevertheless, there are two things which must be borne in mind in this connection. First, that the State subsidy necessary to maintain these services is a drain on our dwindling resources, a burden on the rest of the community, and a brake upon the natural impetus to recovery as far as it exists. In the second place, it has to be remembered that a worker's household which is already supplied with such comforts as adequate bedding, clothing, boots, furniture, etc. can weather a period of a few months on an insurance standard of income, but when the period extends to years instead of months the physical conditions are entirely changed and the psychological reactions wholly different.

For these reasons the present period must be regarded as one in which we are drawing both upon the economic reserves of the nation and the psychological reserves of the people. Before we exhaust either this wealth or this patience it is vitally necessary to discover a means of escape from the depression; a policy which will revitalise the nation with the hope of recovery.

It is the purpose of this book to examine the problems confronting us and to adumbrate a policy of action suitable to the present situation. But it will go further than that; for it will be submitted that any short-term policy of "salvage" work can only be successful if it harmonises with a considered view of the fundamental changes which must be carried out in the structure of our economic system and in the organisations through which alone a comprehensive economic policy can be made effective.

Hysterical proposals of the "do something", "do anything" variety are extremely dangerous in a situation like that of this country at the present time. We have neither the time nor the resources for light-hearted experimentalism. If and when we start out on the road we must be clear as to our destination. A few years ago we might safely have proceeded on the principle of trial and error. To-day it is vitally important to be right. But this realisation of the need for caution will not be regarded as an excuse for doing nothing. The only thing we can conceive of as more dangerous than a mistaken policy is to have no policy at all. For it is surely evident, despite the movements of partial recovery which may occur, that there can be no easy and effortless escape from a situation which results from deep-seated changes in the character and balance of world production and trade, until we have carried out the adjustments in our system which these changes demand.

The old system of "free capitalism", of which Britain was the creator and the pioneer, was a world system. Its conception was that of a world in which each area would devote itself to that form of commodity production for which it was best suited, and exchange its products for the specialised products of other countries in the world market. In theory, at least, it was essentially a complementary, rather than a competitive system of international trade.

In this way it endeavoured to achieve the full economies of the division of labour, and to a large degree it succeeded. The productive power of labour was enormously increased. Man's age-long fight against scarcity was ended and the problem of production solved. It has broken down in face of the problem of distribution, not because there was anything wrong in this conception of co-operative and complementary effort, but because it has come into conflict with equally powerful forces of a non-economic character. The division of the world into nations was not consistent with the welding of the world into a single economic unit. The aggressive acquisitive instincts on which the system relied for its driving force found scope for what might be regarded as their healthy exercise while the world market was expanding and while new areas awaiting capital development and exploitation continued to offer a sphere for individual enterprise and initiative.

As the world became more congested with the spread of industrialism, and when the rate of capital and market expansion was exceeded by the rate of increase in production, the competitive character of the system became more evident and acute. The rival producers in each separate area naturally turned to the use of their State organisation as an additional weapon to aid them in their struggle. Nations changed from being merely political and cultural entities; and economic nationalism became the dominating influence in their councils. The same forces, therefore, which in the early stages of expansion appeared logically to seek the unification of the world, provided in the later stages the impetus towards separation and division. Political nationalism was a fact before economic internationalism was conceived. The remarkable thing is that even the advocates and protagonists of free trade and the expanding world market—a theory which was essentially internationalist—were themselves isolationist and nationalist in their political philosophy. It is even more remarkable to note that in the present-day world we have worked round almost to the completely reverse contradiction. Political and cultural internationalism is to-day at least conceivable (and in fact is in operation in a large field through the League of Nations and other bodies) and it is economic nationalism which now bars the way to world co-operation.

This development of what is called "economic nationalism" is a fact. We may regret it; it is impossible to ignore it. The problems with which we are confronted to-day have their roots in the disequilibrium in world production to which it gives rise. Competition has been intensified with every step forward in the velocity of production. Prices break under the strain of the fierce necessity to keep the machines running and unload their output on the market. Costs of production are cut to a minimum. The more backward nations with a lower standard of life undercut the more highly developed. The machines which enabled man to conquer scarcity now threaten to plunge him deeper and deeper into poverty. These facts constitute the background of our difficulties. It may be that had it not been for the War the speed with which we have run into the production crisis would not have been so great. It is possible that had war been avoided and our attention devoted to these questions as they began to grow more and more acute, some solution of the problems might have been found. But the appalling truth seems to be that the War was itself largely a product of the psychological reactions of statesmen and nations to the economic circumstance which we have described.

Since 1918 we have had superimposed upon this basic economic conflict all the complications of reparations, debts, the new industrialisms of the East and Middle East, for which war provided the impetus, and the whole string of problems—tariffs, subsidies, exchange restrictions, unstable currencies, and the like—arising out of the post-war settlements. In attempting to find an adequate policy for the present day and a theory of the economic system of the future it is essential that we should see these problems, not as isolated and unrelated phenomena, but as different aspects of the same thing, as connected expressions of the basic conflicts which it is our task to solve. The realities of our situation must not be obscured by too polite an interpretation of men's actions and motives. We must face the fact that we do not live in an economic society of orderly conception and altruistic principles. We must realise the essential contradictions of *laissez-faire* even while we may appreciate the energy and drive of a rugged individualism. The policy we are seeking will only be satisfactory if it goes *deep* enough to correct the maladjustments and reconcile the disharmonies from which our problems arise. But, if revolutionary violence is to be avoided, it must also make its appeal to a sufficiently *broad* strip of public opinion to secure the support for its adoption. It must be at once radical and popular.

In order, therefore, that this study may be both objective and practical, the line of approach which we shall adopt will be to seek to discover first what changes are economically necessary and then to discuss the form in which they might be made politically possible.

CHAPTER II

THE WORLD CONFERENCE AND WHY IT FAILED

DURING the greater part of last year, in speeches, in articles in the press, and in a memorandum [1] circulated to Members of Parliament and others, I was urging the acceptance of an interpretation of the deep-seated nature of the crisis which arises out of the analysis briefly indicated in the last chapter. At the same time I put forward suggestions as to the lines on which a solution should be sought, and the structural changes in industrial organisation which would be necessary to such a policy. The following quotation from an article I contributed to the Winter issue of *Service* [2] (the quarterly journal of the Rotary International) will convey an impression of the line of thought which will be examined in greater detail in other sections of this book.

"Our problem, as I see it, is one of the balance of production of separate commodities. It is primarily a production problem. We suffer not from general over-production but from a disproportion or disequilibrium in production. There can be no *general* over-production until all the demands of man have been satisfied. It is true that there are many aggravations of this production problem in the field of politics and high finance. Reparation payments and the shortage of or sterilisation of gold interfere with the normal

[1] *The Next Step*, June 15, 1932.

[2] "Self-Government for Industry," *Service*, Vol. I, No. 4. 1932.

exchange of goods by creating fluctuations in the measure of values or by attempting to take deliveries without making payments. The spread of industrialisation first created the disproportion in production and then gave rise to the tariff barriers, exchange restrictions, and other devices in an effort to protect separate communities from the natural economic consequences.

"These questions will require a political solution, but their relation to the basic problem from which they arise must be seen and understood. An economic policy which deals only with the complications and ignores the primary disease is rather like treating measles by endeavouring to remove the spots.

"But if we are to go to the roots of the problem, two things seem to be essential. First, that we should discover by thorough scientific market research and by political negotiation of commercial arrangements approximately the character and volume of goods we can reasonably expect to sell abroad. This survey should also determine the nature and volume of the imports we take in exchange. Having sought the highest possible level of stable commercial relations with other countries, our task is then clearly one of adapting our internal production to a new equilibrium in which the supply of goods and services will equal demand and, because of correctness in proportion, exchange freely in the home market.

"Such a policy is impossible without the co-operation of industry. Production cannot be planned in relation to estimated demand while industries are organised on competitive lines. *In present circumstances there are no channels through which any economic policy at all can be effectively administered throughout the field of productive effort.* It is for this reason that I regard it as a matter of primary importance to produce an orderly structure in each of our national industries amenable to the authority of a representative directorate conducting the industries as self-governing units in accordance with the circumstances of the modern world.

"The exact method by which this might be achieved —the form of the organisational structure that is— would probably have to be different in different industries. But the common characteristic which must be aimed at is that each national council should be representative both of the geographical and the functional subdivisions of the industry and should be endowed with the authority which would enable it to plan production on the most scientific lines and regulate its output in accordance with estimated demand. The line of approach I would favour is for the Government to request each industry to prepare, within a specified time, a scheme by which the general organisational objective would be achieved. Failing agreement within the industry it would reserve the right itself to negotiate an agreement on correct lines through a committee of industrial advisers.

"With such an organisation, the link between industry and finance and the direction of the flow of investments as advocated by the Macmillan Committee and the F.B.I. would be brought within the sphere of practical politics; industrial self-government could be reconciled with national economic efficiency and political action restricted to its proper sphere in the confident expectation that the problems of production and employment would be adequately dealt with by those familiar with the daily questions which arise."

In order to provide the impulse to achieve this policy and the impetus to an immediate expansion of employment, a short-term policy of monetary reflation through the agency of public works was also advocated. These proposals failed to convince a Government whose attention was concentrated on the coming

World Economic Conference. While they still had hope of international agreement on some form of economic disarmament which, they appeared to believe, would enable the old automatic mechanism of "free capitalism" to function again, any proposal of independent action was looked upon as dangerous or unnecessary. It became evident that until the Conference had completed its discussions no comprehensive policy within the power of this country to carry out on its own initiative would receive consideration.

The Conference is now ended. It has failed in its purpose. And it is vitally necessary that the failure should be recognised and proclaimed. For while there remains a lingering hope that everything will come right of its own accord, or any basis for the belief that a return to the old system is possible as a result of the passing of resolutions or the signing of conventions, no definite, determined and realistic plan of action will be adopted.

The Conference might be regarded, however, as having fulfilled at least this useful function: it has enabled us to test the possibilities of "putting back the clock" in economic, political and social affairs, and has shown clearly that political agreement cannot be built on a basis of economic conflict. This is not to say that the Conference did not, or could not, accomplish anything at all. The fact that it was attended by nearly every nation in the world was in itself an important achievement. It revealed the desire for co-operation and peace; a recognition of the interdependence of nations; and an anxiety to restrain and correct the competitive character of national production and international trade. There was some clarification of the issues involved in currency stabilisation and an effort to provide for consultation between primary producers which may possibly lead to some adaptation of production to demand.

In general, however, the Conference approached its problem on the assumption that if agreement could be secured with regard to stabilisation, tariff reductions, price policies and debt modifications, the larger question of the flow of world trade would solve itself. It was governed by the general assumption that its task was to remove an artificial superstructure of impediments to trade; and that once these were removed the old economic system would function again in the way it had done before. We shall fail to learn the lesson which these discussions contained unless we seek to understand *why* agreement was found to be impossible.

It is suggested that the Conference was studying *effects* rather than *causes*; that tariffs, exchange restrictions, uneconomic prices, currency fluctuations and the like are merely the political devices forced upon each nation in reaction to the market congestion which the spread of industrialism has produced. It is true that the War debts have intensified the production crisis; but had the debtor nations had scope to exercise the increased productivity of the machine, and had the world market been expanding rapidly enough to absorb the increase, even the swollen indebtedness of the War could have been worked off in the course of time.

The size of the debt should be considered in relation to the powers of production. By that test it is doubtful whether the present burden of debt is greater than that we inherited as a legacy of the Napoleonic wars. The crisis did not occur because the productive power of the debtors could not be expanded to make the deliveries, but rather because the creditors were unable to accept payment. They were unable to accept payment for the reasons which have already been indicated. The rate of market expansion has been outstripped by the rate of increase in the power to produce. In other words, the world is equipped to produce more than the world markets will absorb. As a result, the struggle for markets has become more intense. Creditor nations are thus placed in a grave dilemma. They can only accept payment by receiving, in one form or another, the wealth which their debtors produce. To receive it in goods would rob their own nationals of the home market which they have endeavoured to protect; unemployment in the creditor countries would increase; the national industries would decline, and they would lose from their decay as much as they might gain from the receipt of debt. Moreover, as a result of such a policy they would be exhausting the capital accumulations which it had taken years to build up.

It may be said the creditor nations could take payment in gold, but it was precisely the effort to do so which precipitated the crisis from which we are trying to escape. The drain of gold from debtors to ultimate creditors forced one country after another off the gold standard. The fall in the value of the currencies of debtor countries gave them a competitive advantage in world markets. The creditors therefore suffered a loss of their foreign trade, and their effort to compete at the lower price level provided a channel through which the shock of crises was transmitted to their own internal economy. Thus they became involved in the collapse which they had themselves induced. Such, in brief, is the history of the American slump. In these circumstances it was obviously as useless to ask creditors to reduce the tariff barriers which protected the only secure market left to them, as to ask debtors to abandon the exchange restrictions which were forced upon them by the necessity to maintain a foreign trade surplus in order to meet their foreign obligations.

These comments upon the World Economic Conference are made not with the intention of criticising the delegations who attended it, but in order to show how the attempt to secure agreement on the outstanding problems was frustrated by the deeper conflicts which it should have been impossible for statesmen to ignore. It is probable that the Conference will soon be recognised as the last great effort to return to the free market system by the cancellation of what appeared on the surface to be the impediments. We have learned, if we did not know already, to distinguish between the symptoms and the disease; we begin to realise that we are not confronted merely by chance obstacles to recovery subject to the political will of nations, but by problems of growth and change to which our social, political and economic organisation must be adjusted. We must turn our back upon the World Conference, not in a spirit of narrow aggressive nationalism, but as realists, and seek a solution of our problems along other lines. In doing so we must recognise the importance of reconciling national rehabilitation with world co-operation; the two things are not incompatible. In economic affairs we need not be governed by passion. The development of an alternative line of policy would not be helped by a spirit of antagonism to "the foreigner" as such. We cannot detach ourselves from the world we live in as a nation, even if we wished to do so. Our standard of life, our commercial prosperity, our prospects of peace and security will continue to be influenced by the degree of international goodwill which can be engendered. Our policy, therefore, must be one which seeks to improve our own position without inflicting injury upon our neighbours.

CHAPTER III

THE CASE FOR PLANNING

THE idea of planning is slowly but definitely gaining ground as the real nature of the problem now confronting us is revealed. It is a view which arises out of the realities of industrial and commercial life. It has found its adherents not so much among theorists as among those industrialists who see that it is in harmony with what they find it necessary to aim at in the daily conduct of their business. Economic planning is the attempt to regulate production in accordance with effective demand. It is not a new or strange idea. It is, in fact, what every producer must attempt in order to sell his products at a profit rather than a loss. What *is* new is the set of circumstances which requires the co-ordination of the efforts of private individuals and groups to achieve and maintain an equilibrium which in former times could well enough be preserved by an automatic reaction to the indicator of price fluctuation.

The reply which must be made to those who dream of a return to the old days and rebel against any suggestion of organisation—of control, or what they call restriction—is simply that the world has changed, and that such a return is technically, politically and economically impossible. We must live in the world as it is—not as we would like it to be. Industrial and social organisation must fit the circumstances in which its function is to be performed. In modern conditions the system of supply and demand regulated by the price indicator alone—*i.e.* the impetus to production of rising prices and the restraint to production of falling prices—is inadequate.

Apart altogether from the exceptional factors of reparations, debts and conflicting nationalist monetary policies, the system of free, unplanned, capital development by hosts of individuals inadequately informed of each other's activities has always a tendency to produce—and in the present has actually produced—a disequilibrium in production which causes wild variations in price. The bigger the world of investors and producers the wider the fluctuations are likely to become. Large sections of producers become the victims of low prices, and the reduction of their purchasing power drags the whole of industry and commerce into the declining spiral of depression.

During the era of rapid expansion these miscalculations did not produce such disastrous and widespread effects. When the rate of market expansion was more closely related to the increase of production *which was technically and physically possible* the same degree of miscalculation could not occur. In comparing the past with the present, therefore, it must be borne in mind that the important factor is not *the rate of market expansion alone, nor the rate of increased productivity alone, but the rate of market expansion in relation to the rate of increased productivity.*

Bearing that relative factor in mind we are able to see more clearly the basic difficulty confronting the world. It is that for physical and economic reasons—as well as for geographical and political reasons—the relative rate of new capital development has slowed down. New and primitive areas and communities are not being brought so rapidly into the economic system. The limits of the market are more quickly reached. The adjustments of production in response to the falling prices attendant upon depression are more difficult to achieve. The ill direction of the energy of individualistic production would in former times have brought financial loss or ruin only upon the individual producers. But to-day a few firms can so overstock the market as to cause a fall in prices which may spread ruin among all the producers of a particular commodity, not only nationally but it may be throughout the world. Nor are the evil consequences limited to any one class of producers. The fall in their purchasing power injures other industries; and the unemployment of their workers is a burden on the whole of the nation of which they happen to be citizens.

Planning is forced upon us, therefore, not for idealistic reasons, but because the old mechanism which served us when markets were expanding naturally and spontaneously is no longer adequate when the tendency is in the opposite direction. When the world of industrialism was growing up, attention was directed ever outwards to the new areas providing new opportunities. The world has now been more or less encircled by the chain of modern production methods. We are now going back over the ground, as it were; directing our attention to smaller opportunities which may have been missed, and seeking in the areas under our political control some shelter from the chaos of world competition. This political reaction of nations gives rise to the effort to retain by the protection of tariffs or quotas their own home markets for their own producers. Robbed of the opportunities of supplying new expanding markets with the bulk supplies of their mass production, they are forced to seek compensation, and employment for their workers, in the production at home of goods they formerly bought abroad. The system of *protection* is therefore seen to be a natural *by-product* of *the end of effective expansion.*

But protection alone is no solution of the problem. Few countries could manage to maintain their standard of life out of the exploitation of their own natural resources. Interchange of goods is essential to the maintenance of reasonable standards of comfort. Protection must be regarded not as an end in itself but as a preliminary defensive movement. The question is, preliminary to what? How can we contrive that world trade can be carried on on the basis of fair interchange of goods and at the same time protect ourselves from the dislocation of fluctuating and uneconomic prices? Free trade merely means that the markets will go to those who can produce the same quality of goods with the lowest paid labour. Free trade when the period of effective expansion has ended, can only mean competition in wage levels and general labour costs. It presages the triumph of those nations which are the least cultured and the least humane, and the downfall of those people who regard production as a means to life rather than life as a means to production.

The problem to be solved has two aspects—the national and the international. Protection, which, in my view, has meaning only as an aid to planning the development of our national resources, creates the conditions in which the national aspect of the problem can be dealt with. In a later section of this book I hope to show that the organisational structure which we must create to carry on internal production on planned lines, will make it easier for us to deal with the international aspect of the problem; that is, the exchange of home-produced goods and services for the goods and services of other countries.

Disequilibrium in production arises out of the errors and miscalculations of producers in estimating demand and probable supply. The estimation of the likely total of effective demand in any given market is not of itself a very difficult problem. It could be determined accurately enough to avoid at least any very serious dislocation from over-production. The real difficulty lies in the fact that a large number of producers acting separately and individually cannot regulate supply. One individual or group may know nothing of what other individuals and groups are doing and, although the capacity of the market may have been accurately determined by each, the total volume of production may still be in excess of requirements. As a result, intense competition will lower prices to an unprofitable level and thus spread ruin and dislocation in ever-widening circles. The fact is that most producers will be guided by the price indicator, for there is no other guide available. If prices are high they expand their production; and, as the latent productive capacity of many industries is now so great, it is probable the market will be swamped and prices collapse. It is true that this kind of fluctuation has always been in operation; and it may be said, that in former times the dislocation was not very serious, while the healthy bankruptcies which occurred served to keep the balance level between productive capacity and demand. But if we bear in mind the enormously increased *rate* of modern production it will be seen that this factor plus the increase in the *number* of producers, all controlling reserve capacity, makes the danger of miscalculation much more acute in modern times. Indeed, the existence of this danger is clearly proved by the strenuous efforts to create producers' cartels both national and international, which are such a feature of large-scale industry to-day. The industrialists themselves are quite well aware of the difficulty, and have taken these steps in an effort to overcome it.

It may perhaps be argued that if industrialists are aware of the danger, and are given adequate protection in the home market, they can be trusted to take the necessary steps to create a national organisation to regulate supplies and maintain prices at a profitable level. Unfortunately it is not quite so simple as that. For, if they are successful in their efforts and prices are kept at a profitable level, then these prosperous conditions will attract new capital into that form of production; the new firms outside the agreement will set up redundant plant and the old conditions of competitive over-capacity will be recreated. The danger of this occurring is greater when the opportunities for capital investment are reduced. Again, we have to remember the awkward fact that the period of positive or effective expansion is over. (Effective expansion, it will be remembered, is an increase in the rate of market expansion which equals or exceeds the rate of increase in productive capacity.)

We are forced then to the conclusion that two things are necessary for the planning of production in any national unit. (1) It must be adequately protected and (2) regulative powers amounting to monopoly must be granted to efficiently organised and integrated national industries.

If we believe, as we must believe, that a worsening employment situation, and an intensification of depression, will lead to a growth of poverty and discontent and a weakening of the power of Government to relieve distress, then the alternative to bold reconstruction under quasi-monopoly powers may be a deterioration in political conditions which will plunge us into violent social conflict with the risk of social disintegration. The choice is no longer as between industrial *laissez-faire* and monopoly; but between trustification and socialisation, or, it may be, between orderly capitalism and economic and social disorder.

In the last chapter it was stated that the world is equipped to produce more than the world markets will absorb. This statement is a self-evident truth. But there are two observations which have to be made. In the first place, it is an economically ridiculous and a politically dangerous state of affairs. It is ridiculous because millions of people are enduring poverty and hardship as an apparent consequence of potential plenty. It is dangerous because an intelligent populace will not suffer permanently under so painful a paradox. The danger is not that they will destroy merely the system which creates poverty amidst plenty, but that they may be driven in desperation to destroy much that is valuable as well. Until we take action to deal with the economic evil the political danger will exist. We are to-day preparing the ground for violence. We are feeding fanatical revolutionary movements with the material they require. By refusing to speed up the process of social evolution we are making revolution possible and perhaps inevitable.

The second observation is that this economic condition proves the need for planning. It is the evidence which shows how far the economic system is out of gear. It is a condition which results not from general over-production (there can be no general over-production till all the needs of man are satisfied), but from a disequilibrium in the production of goods for exchange. When one commodity is over-produced in relation to all the others its price falls, the purchasing power of its producers declines, and, if the disproportion is great enough, the shock is transmitted from one industry to another by the reduction in effective demand. This is the evil from which our problems arise. It can only be cured, and in future prevented, by the creation of an organisational structure in industry which will bring the individual producers within the control of a central direction capable of determining the quantity of each commodity produced in at least an approximate relation to the market demand.

The principle of quantitative regulation has already been accepted with regard to certain items of our import trade. It is made effective by import quotas for certain food-stuffs. The principle was accepted in order that we might protect our home market from the dislocating consequences of mere cheapness. The same process of reasoning is here being applied to home production whether for home consumption or for export. Quantitative regulation is essential to economic prices and market stability. If this principle is accepted in regard to our import trade, then it must be recognised that the argument is equally powerful when applied to our home production. The over-supply of any commodity produces the same market effects whether it comes from Birmingham or Timbuctoo. Quantitative regulation is the secret of price stability.

The method of achieving it over the whole range of commodities is through the integration of industry and the intelligent direction of production by a central authority for each industry guaranteed against redundancy, duplication and disorderly competition by the grant of monopoly powers in return for the acceptance of certain social responsibilities.

CHAPTER IV

SELF-GOVERNMENT FOR INDUSTRY

THE word monopoly will immediately arouse certain fears and prejudices. It is used deliberately in order that it may be explained. Throughout the whole period of "free capitalism" we have been taught to regard monopolies as organisations deliberately created for the purpose of exploiting consumers by high prices through the maintenance of scarcity. This is rather a one-sided view, and abundant evidence could be quoted to show it has not always been true; yet it can be said that in the circumstances of the past the consumer had no adequate safeguard against high prices artificially maintained by monopoly control except the competition of rival producers.

We are faced then with this choice; either to allow haphazard and unco-ordinated competition to go on producing its wild lurches from normality to depression, or to face the problem of finding a method by which the interests of monopoly-producing organisations can be brought into harmony with the interests of the nation as a whole. At a later stage we will discuss the question as to whether and to what extent it is true that the artificial high prices of scarcity really benefit the producer. It will be submitted that there is such a thing as an efficiency level both of the production and the marketing of goods, and that it is only within very definite limits that the producer can benefit himself by exploiting the consumer, even in the absence of competition.

Before we reach that stage of the argument, however, it is perhaps better for us to consider the full programme of structural reorganisation that is proposed. It will then be seen that the powers of any single monopoly will be limited and restrained if it is operating in a society in which the other functions of production and distribution are similarly organised. A single monopoly in an otherwise competitive society may be able, within the limits of profitability already mentioned, to exploit the producers of its raw material at the one end and the consumers of its finished products at the other. But if the producers of its raw materials are also organised on monopoly lines and the consumers protected by a social organisation for the preservation and expansion of the market, then there is a balance of power by which any tendency to excess can be avoided.

The passage from my article in *Service* for the last quarter of 1932 has already indicated the general character of the new structure of organisation proposed for industry. In a memorandum[1] which I circulated to Members of Parliament and others in June 1932 this proposal was advanced in the following terms:—

(1) "The creation of representative National Industrial Councils for each industry and/or group of industries whose function would be to encourage and assist the efficient co-ordination of purchasing, production, marketing and research, on lines which would enable each industry to evolve towards the highest possible unity of policy and the necessary degree of centralisation of control.

[1] *The Next Step.*

(2) "The creation of an Investment and Development Board representative of

The Government.—Through the Tariff Advisory Committee.

Industry.—Through the National Industrial Councils.

Finance.—Through some such body as the Bankers' Industrial Development Trust with powers and functions enlarged.

"This body would synchronise and relate Political, Industrial and Financial policy to the common object of equilibrium. It would direct investment into the correct channels as advocated in the Macmillan Committee's Report and recently by the Federation of British Industries.[1] It would influence credit policy and direct the efforts of the Councils of Industry to achieve a new internal production balance in relation to the most scientific estimation of market requirements."

In support of this proposal it was stated that:

"Difficult as the task may be, it is certainly impossible to revert to the old system of trial and error in which equilibrium was achieved by the ruin of those who miscalculated demand and by the retreat of investment from the product over-produced. In modern conditions with mass production methods and heavy fixed capital charges, such miscalculation is not a minor accident but a disaster which spreads its consequences throughout the whole system, and drags us through a cycle of depression from whose consequences no section of industry is exempt."

Since that was written nothing has occurred to prove these admittedly drastic changes to be unnecessary. On the contrary, the whole trend of events seems to

1 "A New British Financial Policy." A Report by the Federation of British Industry (1932).

support the view that it is only along some such lines we can find a solution to our problems.

In adopting these proposals we would not be moving into an entirely unknown field. Apart altogether from the various experiments in Public Utility administration, we have had, in recent years, an even more intimate experience of the centralised and co-ordinated management of productive industries. The Electricity Board has carried through an enormous task which is creditable to those associated with it and immensely advantageous to the nation. In 1931 the disorderly, and periodically disastrous, state of organisation in the Mining industry led to the passing of the Mines Act, under which an attempt has been made by the Mines Reorganisation Commission to induce or compel the efficient co-ordination of production at which we are aiming. The London Passenger Transport Act is now in operation. It was forced upon us not by theoreticians but by facts. We now have an organisation at work eliminating the wasteful redundancy and the competitive confusion of London passenger transport and developing an efficient service in accordance with economic and social requirements.[1] In Agriculture we have experimented with the Wheat quota; begun the process of reorganising Pig production and Bacon curing; created a new organisation for the orderly production and marketing of milk, and applied the Agricultural Marketing Act of 1931 to other products.

Each of these steps towards the planning of our economic life has yielded experience in the light of

[1] It is also worth noting that quite recently the four main line railway companies have acquired a controlling interest in Carter Paterson and Pickfords, with the object of co-ordinating the facilities now afforded by those undertakings and by the railway companies themselves.

which more efficient forms of organisation may be evolved. It is not proposed here to go into the merits or demerits of these experiments. They are mentioned merely to indicate that the principles of organisation now advocated for our various national industries are in harmony with the tendency of events. Planning has been admitted to be necessary in regard to Electricity, Coal-mining, Transport and Agriculture. There are few people who would deny the beneficial effects of the action taken under the Electricity Supply Act or the London Passenger Transport Act. In Coal-mining only a very timid and tentative approach has been made and the insufficiency of the planning is demonstrated by the insufficiency of the results. The Agricultural experiments are still perhaps too young to justify even a passing observation, but no intelligent observer could deny that the prospects of stability and prosperity, for those sections of the industry affected, are brighter to-day than they have ever been during the last decade.

A useful summary of the range of these experiments has been published in a Broadsheet [1] issued by the Political and Economic Planning Group and is reproduced on page 30 for the convenience of the reader.

But the full benefits of Planning cannot be obtained if the policy is only partially applied. It would be an entirely false conception of the nature of the problem confronting British industry as a whole to imagine that it can be divided up into separate problems for separate industries, which can be solved bit by bit and industry by industry. Beneficial results can, of course, be obtained and partial planning justified when a particular

[1] "Planning" numbers 5 and 12 published by the Political and Economic Planning Group, 12 Queen Anne's Gate, London, S.W.1.

AGENCIES OF RECONSTRUCTION: SOME RECENT EXPERIMENTS

Name and date of origin.	Present scope.	Progress to date.	Source of revenue.	Area of operation.
1. H.M. Forestry Commission (1919).	A statutory corporation, charged with the production and supply of timber in Great Britain, creates State forests on land purchased or leased and provides grants for planting by local authorities and landowners.	Has acquired over half a million plantable acres and has planted 230,000 acres: much war-time felling still to be made good.	Government grants and trading receipts.	Great Britain only.
2. Electricity Commission (1920).	Preparation of schemes: issue of information and statistics: specified powers of control over electricity undertakings.	Has planned the National Grid and analysed generation and cost of electricity consumed.	Levy on units of electricity sold.	Great Britain only.
3. Central Electricity Board (1927).	Standardisation and bulk supply to distributors of electricity bought from efficient stations: does not undertake distribution to consumers.	Has completed the Grid of 4,000 miles of transmission lines costing £26·7 mns.: standardisation two-thirds finished: normal trading in Central Scotland and Mid-East England began 1/1/1933.	Trading services to repay borrowed capital. State guarantee not used.	Great Britain only.
4. British Broadcasting Corporation (1927).	Monopoly charter for establishment and operation of wireless broadcasting services.	Has organised a system of 21 stations of regional, national and Empire scope, giving regular broadcast programmes to all British countries. Licences increased from 2·3 mns. in 1927 to 5·23 mns. at end of 1932.	10*s.* tax on receiving sets; net amount in 1932 £1·6 mns.	United Kingdom.
5. Traffic Commissioners (1931).	Licensing all public service vehicles for definite times and routes: passenger traffic only.	Elimination of redundant services: improvement of economic status of road transport: co-ordination with railways begun.	Payments from Treasury: receipts go to Road Fund.	Great Britain only.
6. Coal Mines Reorganisation Commission (1931).	Has power to call on coalowners in any area to amalgamate, and in default itself to formulate a scheme.	Has called on coalowners in Fife and Cannock Chase to amalgamate: schemes under discussion for Leicestershire and S. Derbyshire.	Levy on coal output.	Great Britain only.
7. Hops Marketing Board (1932).	Controls sale of hops but not production.	Since operation of the Board wholesale prices have reached a remunerative level and production has increased.	Levy on the crop.	England and Wales.

Name and date of origin.	Present scope.	Progress to date.	Source of revenue.	Area of operation.
8. London Passenger Transport Board (1933).	Ownership and operation of all omnibus, tramway, coach and underground railway services wholly within its area. Participates with main-line railways in pool for suburban traffic.	Unified management of metropolitan passenger transport services and reorganisation of routes began July 1933.	Commercial receipts from traffic.	Greater London.
9. Milk Marketing Board (1933).	Purchase, for resale to distributors and other users, of all milk.	(Just formed.)	Levy on milk handled.	England and Wales. (Separate boards for Scotland.)
10. Pigs Marketing Board (1933).	Participates in all contracts between producers and curers, fixes prices, licenses sale by quantities, provides efficiency services.	(Just formed.)	Levy of 1*s.* 2*d.* per pig cured.	Great Britain. (Separate board for Northern Ireland.)
11. Bacon Marketing Board (1933).	Has power to fix selling price, grades and treatment of British bacon sold to retailers and to require information of all kinds.	(Just formed.)	Levy on pigs cured as No. 10.	Great Britain. (Separate board for Northern Ireland.)

industry is depressed below the level of all the others; when the prices it obtains for its products are exceptionally low, or when it can be shown that the expansion of this particular industry is essential in order to produce a better equilibrium in home production. No criticism is being advanced against policies of that kind which have already been pursued. The expansion of Agricultural production as a separate policy can be justified on grounds of national health, national safety, and as a means of restoring to some degree a better balance between Agriculture and Industry in the national economy. The maintenance of the Steel industry might similarly be justified on grounds of national safety. Such policies could be shown to be wise, in certain circumstances, even if they proved to be expensive. But they cannot be regarded as a sufficient substitute for a comprehensive policy which would benefit industry as a whole and raise the level of production and of demand by the maintenance of an equilibrium which would enable an increased volume of goods and services to exchange for one another in the home market. The interdependency of industries has surely been demonstrated beyond a shadow of doubt. A depression in one industry communicates itself to all the others, because the market is injured by a decline in the purchasing power of any section of the community. This statement is equally true when we reverse its application. That is to say, that the market for the products of one industry can only be fully enhanced by recovery and prosperity in all the other industries. It is for this reason that a *comprehensive* policy of reconstruction is urged.

Now it is obviously as impossible as it would be unwise for the Government itself to attempt the formulation of schemes for the reconstruction of all our industries. It is a task which can only be performed by Industry itself. The field is too wide and the details too complicated for any authority outside the various industries. Moreover, if the planning of our economic life was attempted by any central bureaucratic authority, then a restricting form of bureaucratic imposition would be the result. *The whole intention of the policy here advanced is to achieve planning through self-government as an alternative to bureaucracy.*

The task of reconstruction is not one which is foreign to, or in conflict with, the opinion of the enlightened leaders of Industry. It is a task which they have been attempting to perform themselves. The Amalgamations, Cartels, Producers' Agreements, Centralised Selling Agencies and the like, which have been formed in recent years, are evidence of the fact that industrialists recognise the need of integration, co-ordination, and regulation in the changed circumstances with which they are confronted.[1] These organisations are too numerous to examine in detail here, but it may be helpful to give a few instances of the movement of opinion within industry towards the idea of a central direction which would overcome the disturbing consequences of redundant plant and disorderly production.

In 1930, National Shipbuilders Security, Ltd. was formed with a nominal capital of £10,000 and with borrowing powers up to £3,000,000. The object of this organisation, which resulted from a collective scheme within the industry itself, is to eliminate redundant capacity in British shipyards, and to secure more economic costs by the resultant concentration of production.

Repeated efforts have been made to secure the acceptance of schemes for the reorganisation of the Lancashire Cotton industry. These efforts and the attitude of mind of more enlightened employers was very cleverly summarised by Mr. T. D. Barlow at the Annual Meeting of the Manchester Chamber of Commerce on February 2, 1933.

"Whatever may be the meaning of the much-abused word 'rationalisation', something of the kind is as

[1] Nationalisation and unification of all the railway companies in Great Britain was discussed by Mr. William Whitelaw, chairman of the L.N.E.R., in his address as president of the Institute of Transport, October 9, 1933.

"National management of the railways would prove, I do not doubt, ruinous to both passenger and industrial transport; but national ownership with management completely divorced from political influence is not impossible. It cannot be dismissed from consideration for all time because of the prejudice attached to the name of nationalisation."

necessary and desirable in the industry as it has ever been. . . . The day can never return when Lancashire will occupy the happy position (as in the past) of being virtually unchallenged as the principal source of supply for the world's requirements in cotton goods, and if we are to make the best of what the future has in store for us, some reshaping of our internal structure is a primary necessity. In the earlier part of my term of office I was associated with the advocacy of certain plans designed to bring about a controlled and orderly contraction in the productive capacity of the Cotton industry. . . . I still think that internal reorganisation of the Cotton trade is inevitable, whether it is brought about by conscious planning or by the painful process of piecemeal disintegration followed by independent reconstruction."

The report of the Government Committee of Inquiry into the conditions and prospects of the Cotton trade (appointed August 1, 1929) stated:

"After making all allowances for the disadvantages which have their causes outside the Cotton industry, we are satisfied from the evidence laid before us that the British Cotton industry has failed to adapt its organisation and methods to changed conditions. . . . The industry, consisting of a series of sharply defined sections, mutually independent of one another, and within each section consisting of a large number of firms in competition with one another, finds it difficult to consent to common action for the good of the whole."

With regard to the Steel industry, it will be remembered that the Protection granted to this industry was conditional upon such reorganisation as would safeguard the interests of the Steel-using industries. A Committee of the industry was set up by Sir George May, as Chairman of the Import Duties Advisory

Committee, to consider plans of reorganisation. A scheme has since been drafted and has received the approval of the National Committee. This scheme proposes that the British Iron and Steel industry should be organised on the basis of a number of approved Associations, each dealing with a group of similar products, and a central body co-ordinating the Associations and incorporated either under Royal Charter or under the Companies Act, called the Iron and Steel Corporation of Great Britain. Its functions would include the supervision of the Associations in all matters of general policy to secure the orderly progress of the industry; to promote desirable amalgamations; to prevent unnecessary duplication of plant; to secure the co-operation of the Associations in promoting the export trade; and by agreement to provide for central purchasing, common marketing and research.

Another interesting indication of the trend of opinion is contained in the speech delivered by Sir Ernest Gowers, K.C.B., K.B.E., Chairman of the Coal Mines Reorganisation Commission, to the Cardiff Business Club on February 24, 1933. Discussing the question of amalgamations he said:

"The question is whether a process of this sort can do what is needed? Can it enable the industry to equate supply to demand at the lowest cost of production and distribution? Can it stop weak selling and wanton price cutting? It is only necessary to put this question in order to suggest a reply—perhaps at first rather a disturbing one—that a policy of amalgamation cannot by itself do these things unless the amalgamations are very big, in the aggregate, all-embracing.[1]

[1] It is reported in the *Manchester Guardian*, September 8, 1933: "An 'agreement of constitution' has been drawn up by the West

"I believe amalgamations to be vitally necessary to the industry, but that is because I do not see how it can be set right without them, not because I think it can be set right by them alone. They are not the final goal, but they are a means to an end. Not that I under-rate their intrinsic importance to efficiency. There must be an optimum size of unit, a size that will secure the admitted benefits of large-scale control without being too big for the control to be efficient.

". . . the industry cannot—as it seems to me—work out its ultimate salvation, in whatever way that is to be done, without first reducing the number of independent units of which it consists. Every ambitious attempt at co-operation has so far foundered on the same rock; there are too many people whose agreement is necessary. I believe myself that what we really want ultimately is not only amalgamations but also a looser form of co-operation over an area wider than the industry is willing to take as its unit of production. I do not think this can be done except by building a ground floor of amalgamations first and adding this looser form of wider co-operation as an upper storey. In other words, it would mean grouping the units of production into much bigger associations—call them cartels or what you will—with two main purposes. One purpose would be to co-operate in selling and distribution. The other would be to exercise a general control over the development of the area and to share the expense of buying and closing mines which no single unit might think it worth while to acquire because it could not be sure enough of getting their trade. And there may be many useful subordin-

Yorkshire Federation providing for the closing down of redundant mines, the transfer of the permissible output under the quota scheme to other mines, the purchase of mines, the co-ordination of marketing, and the regulation of prices, even to the extent of a central selling scheme. These objects are to be achieved without any degree of financial amalgamation."

ate purposes. I do not claim any novelty for the suggestion of a two-storey organisation of this sort. It has been proposed before by people in the industry with a much better title to make suggestions than I have. My excuse for putting it in my Commission's shop-window must be that it is only right that I should say what form of reorganisation we have in view in laying our plans. Even if one's proper task is confined to building the ground floor of a structure, it is wise to draw an elevation of the whole before setting to work."

In their effort to achieve orderly production and marketing, industrialists are hampered and frustrated by two main obstacles.

First, their rate of progress is too often limited to that at which the most backward and stubborn is prepared to move. A minority of "rugged individualists" may arrest the progress which the great majority have recognised to be essential. But even if the obstacle of a recalcitrant minority is removed, they are confronted with a second difficulty. If, as a result of wise leadership and co-operative effort, an agreement is reached by which stable orderly production and profitable sales can be maintained, then these conditions attract fresh entrants to the industry; redundant plant is set up by the new producer outside the agreement, duplication of production is again begun, and the old competitive and disorderly conditions are recreated. This is exactly what has been happening as a result of our recent adoption of Tariffs, and advocates of Protection are, strangely enough, pointing to the new factories which have been established as if there could be no doubt that such a result was beneficial and desirable. Government spokesmen have quoted with pride the results of the Board of Trade Survey of Industrial Development in 1932, which shows—

(*a*) 646 new factories, employing 44,750 people were established in 1932. 166 factories were extended and 355 factories were closed down.

(*b*) Of the new factories, 144 were concerned with clothing, 108 with textiles, 65 with engineering, 51 with iron and steel processes, 55 with timber, while other trades involved include bricks, chemicals, non-ferrous metals, leather, paper and mining products.

(*c*) Of the new factories, 122, employing about 8,500 people, were established by or with the assistance of foreign concerns.

These figures relate to factories employing 25 or more workers. The total number of new factories established by or with the assistance of foreign concerns (including those employing less than 25 workers) from November 1931 to April 1933 was 254.

Is it correct to regard this development as an unmixed blessing? Are these new factories necessary? Are there not a great many industries, such as Textiles, Iron and Steel, Engineering, Mining, etc., where the plant and equipment existing in 1931 were more than adequate to the improved demand of 1932? A glance at the Census of Production figures of separate establishments in each industry would lead one to believe that most of our industries are already overcrowded with separate units and redundant plant. This influx of new producing units from abroad merely transfers chaos from overseas to the home market. It increases the difficulties of those industries which have been striving to secure by amalgamation or by federation a more orderly allocation of production and more stable market conditions for their products. At the moment this aspect of the case is obscured by the benefits which Tariff policy is conferring. Its full importance will be realised at a later stage.

But this is a digression. We were discussing the difficulties with which industry is confronted in its effort to carry through reconstruction. The more progressive leaders may find their efforts frustrated by a recalcitrant minority, or, if they succeed in establishing stable and orderly production and marketing conditions, new producers outside the agreement will be attracted to the industry and the old competitive redundancy will be recreated.

It is in this connection that Government assistance is required. The Government could invite each industry by majority vote to submit its scheme for the integration of the industry into a national unit subject to a suitable central control.[1] In the interests of the nation as a whole it ought to place a time limit on the discussions and reserve the right itself to prepare a scheme if the industry fails to respond. When the scheme has been formulated and the National Council for the industry appointed, then the Government should confer on that authority the necessary statutory powers to carry through the scheme of integration and thereafter to preserve stability by the exercise of regulative powers.[2]

[1] Apart from other consideration, statutory authority would almost certainly be required in nearly every scheme of industrial reorganisation in order to overcome legal difficulties arising from the complicated rights and standing of different classes of share and debenture owners, and thus obviate unnecessary obstruction and delay.

[2] In an article which he contributed to the *Manchester Guardian* on March 10, 1933, Mr. Lennox Lee, Chairman of the Calico

These Councils would be representative of the functional and geographical subdivisions of the industry and their authority would enable them to create the channels through which co-ordination and direction could most efficiently be maintained. There would be no external interference with the conduct of the industry. Each industry or group of industries would be regarded as a self-governing unit. The elimination of the competitive scramble and confusion would enable it to serve the national interests by serving its own.

Representatives of these Councils would be brought together in an Economic Council which was described in the quotation on page 27 as an Investment and Development Board. There they would be in contact with representatives of Finance and of Government, and able to make representations and discuss national monetary or political policy in so far as it affected the industries of the country. Such an organisation obviously opens up possibilities of national co-ordination never before possible. In the next chapter we will examine in detail the functions of this Central Economic Council.

Printers Association, gave powerful support to a strikingly similar view to that which was expressed in my memorandum *The Next Step* in June 1932. He said:

"If some form of industrial self-government could be devised along the lines of an Industrial Council of practical men—men with foresight and world-wide trading experience—with representatives of labour and possessing statutory powers, many of the difficulties which at present confront most industries would become less formidable. Other industries in this country (not only the Cotton industry) are suffering from the lack of authoritative leadership which such councils could give. If rightly constituted and with an efficient personnel they would command the confidence of those dependent on the industry, and the application of such a system would not only facilitate national co-ordination but would also provide a stepping-stone to international industrial co-operation."

The foregoing description of the Industrial Councils is intended merely to convey a conception of their scope and character. It is obviously impossible to do more than lay down the general principles of organisation and unified control. The details of the structure would have to be adapted to the peculiar needs of each industry by those who are familiar with the daily problems confronting it. Indeed it is an important aspect of these proposals that political interference would be reduced to the minimum. The politician is concerned with the general principles of economic organisation, and that only because the conditions of the present-day world are such that social welfare and national stability and security have come to depend so completely on economic policy. The social problems of unemployment and poverty, for instance, cannot be considered apart from the general economic conditions which create them; and, as it has been submitted, the economic conditions cannot be dealt with until there is an ordered structure of industry through which the treatment can be made effective.

The attitude of mind in which these proposals have been advanced has recently been summarised in admirable terms by the present Minister of Transport, Mr. Oliver Stanley.

Speaking at Manchester on September 26, 1933, he said:

"To assume that we must wait for a return of the old conditions was to cherish a dangerous fallacy. He believed that a considerable part of the depression we have suffered since the War had occurred from a quite natural desire on the part of those who knew the old days to get back to as close an approximation to those old days as they could."

After remarking that the emphasis had passed from production to consumption, he continued:

"It would be fatal if we had no real idea on which to work and were simply pushed one way or another according to the demand of immediate problems."

Speaking of the need for "planned industry" "in the new conditions" he said:

"The relationship we have to find lies somewhere between the complete non-interference of the last century and the complete interference of the socialist State. And I want to see that Government interference carried through with the least possible interference with private initiative and private incentive to success.

"*We have heard a great deal in the past about protection for minorities; he was not sure whether the function of Government in the future would not be protection of majorities; whether it was not going to be the duty of Government to protect the majority of an industry which came to a common desire to put its house in order and regulate its production against the inroads of rapacious and irresponsible minorities.*"

It has already been said that the formulation of schemes for the reconstruction of our industries is too complicated and difficult a task for any single authority outside of the industries to accomplish. The expert knowledge of owners and technicians within each industry must be enlisted in the formulation of schemes which are at once adequate and workable.

There need be no fear that such assistance would not be obtainable. Even the most ill-organised and intractable industries are producing leaders who understand the need for moving with the times. These men are genuinely anxious to modernise the methods of production and management. They would welcome the statutory assistance which it is proposed to offer them. They would co-operate loyally in the preparation of plans which were designed to serve simultaneously the real interests of the industry in which they are employed and the interests of the nation as a whole.

Nevertheless, for the explanatory purposes of this book, it is perhaps necessary to venture a little further into an examination of how the principles of integration might be applied.

Practical men now engaged in the conduct of industry or commerce may admit the validity of the theoretical argument but doubt the possibility of applying it. They will want to know how many industries there are, what groupings they fall into, the number of workers affected, the value of their net output, the geographical distribution of plant, and the degree of co-ordination which has already been established.

The Summary of the preliminary reports of the Fourth Census of Production (1930) contains a great deal of information in handy form which would enable the reader to examine the problem in greater detail than is possible here.

For the purposes of the 1930 Census, industrial production was divided into 120 industries. Returns were not required from firms that employed an average of ten or fewer persons in that year. It is estimated that these small firms accounted for about 5 per cent. of the net output of productive industry and about 6 per cent. of the total number of persons employed in industries covered by the Census.

The returns received covered firms employing an

aggregate of 6,784,109 persons, of whom 6,099,553 were operatives and 684,556 were administrative, technical and clerical staff.

In the Census Report these industries are classified in 17 groups. In the following table I have included opposite each group the information which seems to be relevant to what we are discussing here.

	Number of Establishments.	Net Output.	Average Number of Persons Employed.
		£ million.	Thousand.
Non-metalliferous Mining Products	963	16·3	58·7
Bricks, Pottery and Glass	1,872	31·0	174·7
Chemicals	1,764	70·1	175·1
Iron and Steel	3,444	87·3	470·4
Engineering and Shipbuilding	4,398	156·5	733·7
Vehicles	2,762	60·7	272·3
Non-ferrous Metals	1,376	22·8	103·0
Textiles	6,964	134·8	963·9
Leather	819	9·9	44·9
Clothing	6,853	70·9	446·4
Food, Drink and Tobacco	6,896	179·0	447·3
Timber	3,578	28·8	154·1
Paper, Printing and Stationery	4,232	98·8	360·4
Miscellaneous	1,342	36·9	146·5
Building and Contracting	Not available	88·1	452·1
Mines and Quarries	,,	153·5	1,010·1
Public Utility Services, Local Authorities and Government Depts.	,,	186·4	770·5
Grand Total	—	1,431·8	6,784·1

The 120 industries which these groups represent account for the whole of the productive industries in the country apart from Agriculture, Transport and Distribution.

For the convenience of the reader the following list of the separate industries within the industrial groups covered by the Census is taken from the *Board of Trade Journal* of February 16, 1933.

LIST OF INDUSTRIES COVERED BY THE CENSUS OF PRODUCTION

Industrial Groups

Non-metalliferous Mining Products:

Coke and By-Products and Manufactured Fuel.
Cement.
Building Materials.
Manufactured Abrasives.

Bricks, Pottery and Glass:

Brick and Fireclay.
China and Earthenware.
Glass.

Chemicals:

Chemicals, Dyestuffs and Drugs.
Fertiliser, Disinfectant, Glue, etc.
Explosives and Fireworks.
Paint, Colour and Varnish.
Seed Crushing.
Oil and Tallow.
Soap, Candle and Perfumery.
Starch and Polishes.
Match.
Petroleum Refining.
Ink, Gum and Sealing-wax.

Iron and Steel:

Iron and Steel (Blast Furnaces).
Iron and Steel (Smelting and Rolling).
Wrought Iron and Steel Tubes.
Iron Foundries.
Chain, Nail, Screw and Miscellaneous Forgings.
Tinplate.
Wire.
Tool and Implement.
Cutlery.
Needle, Pin, Fish-hook, Button and Metal Smallwares.
Hardware, Hollow-ware, Metallic Furniture and Sheet Metal.
Small Arms.

Engineering and Shipbuilding:

Mechanical Engineering.
Electrical Engineering.
Shipbuilding.

Vehicles:

Motor and Cycle (Manufacturing).
Motor and Cycle (Repairing).
Railway Carriage and Wagon Building.
Carriage, Cart and Wagon.
Aircraft.

Non-ferrous Metals:

Non-ferrous Metals (Smelting, Rolling and Casting):
Copper and Brass.
Lead, Tin, Aluminium and other Non-Ferrous Metals.
Gold and Silver Refining.
Finished Brass.
Plate and Jewellery.
Watch and Clock.

Textiles:

Cotton Spinning.
Cotton Weaving.
Woollen and Worsted.
Silk and Artificial Silk.
Jute.
Hemp and Linen.
Engine and Boiler Packing and Asbestos.
Roofing and Flax Felts.
Coir Fibre, Horsehair and Feather.
Hosiery.
Lace.
Rope, Twine and Net.
Elastic Webbing.
Canvas Goods and Sack.
Flock and Rag.
Textile Finishing.
Packing.

Leather:

Fellmongery.
Leather.
Saddlery, Harness, Travelling Bags and Leather Goods.

Clothing:

Clothing.
Hat- and Cap-making.
Glove-making.
Boot and Shoe.
Fur.
Umbrella and Walking-stick.

Food, Drink and Tobacco:

Grain Milling.
Cattle, Dog and Poultry Foods.
Bread and Biscuit.
Sugar and Glucose.
Cocoa and Sugar Confectionery.
Bacon Curing and Sausage.
Preserved Foods.
Fish Curing.
Butter, Cheese, Condensed Milk and Margarine.
Brewing and Malting.
Spirit Distilling.
Spirit Rectifying, Compounding and Methylating.
Aerated Waters, Cider, Vinegar, British Wine, etc.
Wholesale Bottling.
Tobacco.
Ice.

Timber:

Timber (Sawmilling, etc.).
Wooden Crates, Cases, Boxes and Trunks.
Coopering.
Furniture and Upholstery.
Cane and Wicker Furniture and Basketware.

Paper, Printing and Stationery:

Paper.
Wall Paper.
Manufactured Stationery.
Printing and Publication of Newspapers and Periodicals.
Printing, Bookbinding, Stereotyping, Engraving, etc.
Cardboard Box.
Pens, Pencils and Artists' Materials.

Miscellaneous:

Rubber.
Musical Instruments.
Linoleum and Oilcloth.
Ivory, Horn Picture Frame and Fancy Articles.
Brush-making.
Scientific Instruments, Apparatus and Appliances (including Cinematograph Film Printing).
Sports Requisites.
Games and Toys.
Incandescent Mantles.

Building and Contracting.

Mines and Quarries:

Coal Mines.
Slate Quarries.
Non-metalliferous (other than Slate) Quarries, including Oil-shale Mines.
Metalliferous Mines and Quarries.
Salt Mines, Brine Pits and Salt Works.

Public Utility Services:

Waterworks Undertakings.
Gas Works Undertakings.
Electricity Undertakings.
Local Authorities.
Railway Companies.
Tramway and Light Railway Companies.
Canal, Dock and Harbour Companies.

This list enables us to see clearly the scope of our task in the whole of productive industry outside Agriculture, Transport and Distribution.

In some of the groups it may be that certain industries would find it convenient to coalesce for the creation of National Industrial Councils; in others there might have to be further subdivision; but if we take the list as it stands, it would appear that from 100 to 120 Councils would probably cover the whole field of industrial activity.

The remarkable thing about this analysis is the relatively small number of bodies required for such a vitally important structure of organisation. When it is compared with the 1,850 Local Rating Authorities or the six hundred constituencies electing members to Parliament, it will be seen that no great difficulty need be anticipated in maintaining the necessary contacts.

In proposing the formation of National Industrial Councils for each industry it must be clearly understood that no dogmatic principle of amalgamation of the numerous establishments now under separate ownership is being laid down. Undoubtedly the unnecessary duplication of ownership units would tend to disappear as each National Council set about the task of organising its own industry. The wasteful redundancy of plant would have to be eliminated, but whether this was done by amalgamation, federation, or some other form of producers' agreement would be a matter for the industry itself to decide. The centralisation of control together with the alertness of the Economic Council representing users' and consumers' interests would produce the efficient form of organisation suitable to the particular trade.

Each of these Councils, as has been said, would be represented on the Economic Council, which would be a kind of Industrial Parliament. These representatives would be called together periodically to discuss the general principles of economic policy and report, or advise, upon the problems confronting them and the effect of policy on the productive industries they represented.

For the purposes of carrying on the continuous survey of economic conditions and performing the executive tasks of the Economic Council a smaller body would, however, be required. In the formation of such an Executive Council we might follow the example of industrial organisations which now exist, such as the Federation of British Industries, the National Federation of Employers organisations, the Trades Union General Council and other such bodies. These organisations are faced with the same task of representing each section of industry on their Executive bodies and they do so by a group system.

There is an additional reason for the grouping of industries in accordance with the relation of their functions in the organisation which we are discussing. In the case of industries related to one another by the vertical processes of working up the raw material to the finished article ready for the final consumer, there would have to be a close co-ordination of the policy each was pursuing. A study of the list of industries by experts would no doubt result in the determination of suitable groupings.

The industries in each group could make their own arrangements for consultation and co-ordination of policy, and they could combine to elect a member to the Executive body of the Economic Council. These groups would probably be differently arranged from the list quoted from the *Board of Trade Journal*. This list was divided into 17 groups exclusive of Agriculture, Transport, Distribution and Finance. It is reasonable to suppose, however, that the number of groups under the new arrangement would be similar. This would give 21 groups, and, with the addition of representatives of Economists, Scientific Research, Labour, and Government, would not be too large a body.

There may be some who will regard such an organisation as far too complicated and who may doubt whether it could ever function in the way we have envisaged. Before passing that criticism upon the proposals, regard should be taken of the fact that the Federation of British Industries is a standing example of how such a form of organisation does work. In the statement of the "Objects and Work" of the F.B.I. the following claim is made.

"In the United Kingdom the F.B.I. is organised both geographically and functionally, being divided (*a*) into 13 districts, each in charge of a resident secretary who is responsible to his local committee; and (*b*) into 24 industrial groups. It can, therefore, with equal facility, at any given moment obtain the views of all manufacturers in one centre, or of all members of the same trade throughout the country. Its reputation and standing ensure that these views shall be heard and respected."

FEDERATION OF BRITISH INDUSTRIES

Industrial Group Representives

		Sub-Groups or Sections.
Group 1.	Mining, Quarrying and Allied Trades	9
Group 2.	Mechanical Engineering	37
Group 3.	Shipbuilding, Marine Engineering, Constructional Steel Work and Allied Trades	3
Group 4.	Electrical Engineering	4
Group 5.	Iron, Steel and Allied Trades	12
Group 6.	Textiles	17
Group 7.	Glass and Clay products	4
Group 8.	Printing, Printing Ink Manufacturers, Typefounders, Process Workers and Allied Trades	6
Group 9.	Chemicals, Fertilisers and Explosives	5
Group 10.	Food-stuffs and Tobacco	13
Group 11.	Agriculture	2
Group 12.	Building Trades	2
Group 13.	Rubber and Asbestos	3
Group 14.	Public Utility	14
Group 15.	Miscellaneous	16
Group 16.	Non-ferrous Metals	6
Group 17.	Oils and Fats (including Soap, Candles and Margarine), Oil Seed crushing and its By-products	5
Group 18.	Paper-making, Manufacturing Stationery, Envelope-making, Paper-Bag-making, Box-making and Allied Trades	8
Group 19.	Banking and Insurance	2
Group 20.	Woodworking	6
Group 21.	Cutlery, Jewellery, Electroplate and Allied Trades	11
Group 22.	Brewing, Distilling and Allied Trades	4
Group 23.	Fisheries	2
Group 24.	Leather and Allied Trades	5

CHAPTER V

THE CO-ORDINATION OF FINANCIAL, INDUSTRIAL AND POLITICAL POLICY

In passing to a consideration of the functions of the central economic organisation, the situation which we have to visualise is one in which disorderly production and competitive selling have been eliminated by the operation of the Industrial Councils. Each national industry has achieved a corporate unity; the separate industries in the group, or the sub-sections of each industry, may be under their own management, but their activities will be co-ordinated and directed by the protective supervision of the Council under whose auspices they come. The market, let us suppose, is being studied scientifically and industry has been organised to ensure that each plant, constructed with a view to its specialised task within the industry, is able to maintain its production at what is called the "efficiency" level. By these means, not only has anarchy been banished from the market but an instrument has been forged by which the economic activities of each section of the nation can be harmonised with the general economic policy of the nation as a whole.[1]

It will be remembered also that we have agreed to assume for the moment that the problem of our trade

[1] The Federation of British Industries, in a memorandum to the Government dated October 12, 1933, with regard to the negotiation of Commercial Treaties says, "This Federation believes that the economic recovery of this country largely depends on the closest possible co-operation between Government and Industry."

relationship with the rest of the world has been satisfactorily dealt with, and that our new system is immune from the dislocating effects of competitive imports. In a later chapter of this book we shall endeavour to justify that assumption. But, as has already been said, it will be easier to explain the proposals to be advanced in that connection when the internal structure is clearly understood.

To complete our description of the organisation, something more must be said about the Industrial Development Board—or, as it might perhaps better be named, Central Economic Council. It will be composed of representatives of each Industrial Council; representatives of Banking and Finance; representatives of Labour; and the Executive heads of the Import Duties Advisory Committee. There might usefully be added to this list a small group of Economists, capable of advising on the wider aspects of economic policy; and a group of Scientists and Technicians able to supply expert knowledge with regard to scientific invention and research. Such an organisation, representing as it would those responsible for the performance of all the vital economic tasks of the nation, should, it is submitted, sit under the chairmanship of a member of the Cabinet in close contact with the Prime Minister, probably the President of the Board of Trade, or a special minister, devoting the whole of his attention to this work. The Ministers of Transport and of Agriculture, whose work would come within the scope of the Economic Council's discussions, should both be members of it.

It is particularly necessary at this point to make a reference to the Ministry of Agriculture. The form of organisation which has been proposed for industry brings the various units in an industry together as producers; the structure is built up from the *production* end. Such a form of organisation would probably be quite inappropriate for Agriculture. It would be difficult to obtain the necessary cohesion amongst the scattered agricultural community, and the control and direction of production could not be so easily undertaken by a central council for the industry. It seems clear that the line of approach to orderly Agricultural production and marketing is that which has already been adopted under the various marketing schemes. For this reason it is essential that the Ministry of Agriculture should be regarded as the authority through which the general policy should be applied in so far as it concerns that industry. Nevertheless, it is important that agriculturists should be represented as producers; and, despite the fact that policy would still be made operative through the Minister, a Council for Agriculture could still perform a useful function and take its part in the general economic organisation of the country which is here envisaged. It is perhaps worth remarking that a Council of Agriculture is already in existence.

We must now consider what would be the relation between this Central Economic Council and Parliament. Some fears may have been aroused that such a structure of functional representation might become a rival to the democratic institutions of Parliamentary government. It cannot be too strongly stated that there is no such intention and indeed no such danger in the organisation proposed. It is in no way inconsistent with Parliamentary government to build an organisation by which Parliament can be advised on industrial problems and through which the policies it may discuss can be carried out. At present a great part of the discussions in Parliament on economic questions must remain just "talk." If Parliament does not control the economic operations which it is discussing, and if it is regarded as unwise that it should do so, then there is little prospect of it correcting the disequilibrium to which these operations may give rise. It has neither the power nor the machinery for this purpose.

For the Socialist this argument may not hold good. If one is contending that the State should own and operate industry, then one has a logical view of how the discussions in Parliament could be made operative. But if one is seeking a method by which private ownership may be reconciled with public policy, then, if we are going to discuss these subjects at all, we require an organisation through which the policy arrived at can be applied. The economic organisation proposed is not intended to usurp any of the functions of Parliament. It will be available for expert advice. It will be able to speak with a knowledge of the facts. Parliament will, however, be able to devolve on to it tasks and functions which Parliament cannot, in any case, itself perform.

In order that the functions of the Central Economic Council may be explained, it is necessary to bear in mind not only the new conditions of production which will result from the regulative work of the Industrial Councils as indicated in the opening sentences of this chapter, but also part of the argument, relating to the *nature* of a production crisis, already advanced.

It has been stated that in a world highly skilled in the *exchange* of goods there can be no general overproduction until all the wants of man have been satisfied. But the exchange of goods and services can only proceed smoothly and efficiently so long as the goods and services are being produced in quantities which equal demand. For every seller there must be a buyer; but the consuming power of the buyer depends on his being able to dispose of his own product of goods or services in exchange. Or, to put it in another way, we are all *both* buyers and sellers. Our power to buy is limited by our power to sell. It follows, therefore, that the conditions of economic prosperity depend upon the production of goods and services in the quantities which enable them all to exchange for one another. *It is to the achievement and maintenance of this equilibrium that the Economic Council would devote its attention.*

What, then, are the factors which threaten this production equilibrium on which our prosperity depends? In answering that question we shall cover the principal subjects likely to engage the attention of the Economic Council.

Imports.—In the first place, it is threatened by unregulated competitive imports which may drive down prices, and therefore wages, in sections of our home industry and, by the reduction in purchasing power thus created, spread disturbance throughout the whole structure. The Council would make recommendations by which this danger could be checked or avoided through a system of regulation which we shall discuss in Chapter VII.

Over-production.—In the second place, as much of the early argument has been devoted to proving, equilibrium is most seriously endangered by an over-production of certain commodities, which, by reducing the prices at which they are sold, may cause loss to the owners and unemployment among the workers in the industry concerned. Again, by the resulting fall in purchasing power other productive industries become involved. Against this danger we have already erected the system of co-ordinated production. In the new conditions, therefore, it would be unlikely to occur; but if for some unforeseen reason it should happen, the Economic Council would consider action to check its consequences and nurse the system past the danger-point of threatening crisis.

Savings and Investment.—In the third category of dangers we must consider the question of Savings and Investment. This subject is the most intricate and, in a review of the Economic Council's functions, perhaps the most important. In the production of any commodity there is distributed in the form of wages, salaries, rent, interest, profit, etc., sufficient purchasing power to buy back the commodity on the open market. That is to say, the *price* of the article is equal to the total of all these costs or charges. The total purchasing power available is, therefore, equal to the total price of goods and services produced. But the people who receive this purchasing power may not spend it all; they may save part of it against old age, sickness, holidays, the education of their children, the purchase of property, or with the object of providing for their children and dependents in the event of death.

The effect of this is, that, to the extent to which they save, purchasing power is withheld from active demand. If nothing further happened, then it will be obvious that the number of commodities coming on to the market would exceed the demand for them; because, although the necessary purchasing power had been distributed, it was not being fully used by the people possessing it for the satisfaction of their current needs. But something further does happen. The thrifty people who are saving do not, in these days, hoard their money in a chest under their beds; they put it in a Bank for safe-keeping, or they invest it by purchasing securities. Now, if these savings are being invested in real Capital extension—that is to say, if the people with whom it is invested or the banks in which it is deposited are relending it to people who want to build new factories, houses, railways, etc.—then, although the original owner is *saving* it, somebody else is *spending* it.

As long as that happens there is merely a *transference* of purchasing power taking place and no fall in the total entering into effective demand. But when the two operations get out of balance; when the rate at which money is being *spent* on investment goods—*i.e.* factories, houses, railways, etc.—is exceeded by the rate at which it is being *saved*, then more goods are being produced than are being purchased and we run into the old danger of falling prices and general economic dislocation.

It will be seen, therefore, that the maintenance of this balance is vital to stability. Obviously it is impossible to dictate to a multitude of "savers" how much they should save. The action which must be taken is to regulate "investment" in accordance with savings. This operation can usually be achieved by bank policy. If money is plentiful—that is, if the deposits are growing—the banks lend it more cheaply and thus encourage investment. If money is scarce—that is, if the deposits are falling—the banks charge more to the borrower and thus check investment.

The real difficulty arises when there are no profitable opportunities for investment—or insufficient profitable opportunities to use up the idle balances.

It is in this sphere that the Economic Council can help. It must ensure through its financial representatives that general financial policy is directed towards the stability of prices. It must find new avenues for the investment of savings, assist and encourage industries which, in their opinion, it would be in the national interest to expand; and if necessary urge the adoption of public works programmes at times when such a policy is necessary to preserve the stability of the market until the balance between savings and investment has been restored.

This is an inadequate summary of the intricate operations involved in connection with the whole question. It is a subject which would require a book to itself, and the present writer makes no pretence of being qualified to write such a book. Nevertheless, it is not difficult to see the importance of the task, and it has been clearly demonstrated by others [1] that this regulation is not only possible but indeed imperative. The Economic Council would have at its disposal the expert knowledge and the necessary machinery for its performance.

Production and Consumption.—The fourth subject which must come under review by the Economic Council is related to that which we have just been discussing. With every increase in the total volume of production there is likely to be an increase in the volume of savings. And in modern conditions of mass production one can imagine a stage of development being reached when the opportunities—indeed the possibilities—of investing the surplus in new capital

[1] The reader who desires to study this subject will find it dealt with from different angles in the writings of Keynes, Hobson, Hayek and others.

investment cannot keep pace with our increased power to produce. It may seem fantastic even to imagine such a situation while bearing in mind the slums waiting to be cleared, the poverty of great masses of our people—considered in relation to the potential productive capacity of modern industry—the schools and houses which might be built, the cultural opportunities to be extended, and the amenities which might be created by the expenditure of labour. But in thinking of this possibility, and the time likely to elapse before it becomes a pressing question, regard must be had to the hours of labour. If we all worked ten or twelve hours a day the problem would be brought closer. If we worked six hours a day it becomes more remote.

These observations have been made in order to draw attention to the fact that under the system of regulation and order we have envisaged *the reduction of the hours of labour becomes "practical politics" for the first time.* (This is still on the assumption, of course, that we are able to deal with the problem of our foreign trade.) If the Economic Council finds that savings have increased beyond the rate at which investment can conveniently take place, it may be taken as an indication, in the new circumstances of industrial life, that the incomes of the people are in excess of their requirements. It would be possible for the Economic Council to deal with this situation by one of *two* methods. It could recommend an increase of expenditure on Public Works, and thus take workers from the production of commodities for exchange and employ them in the extension of amenities for social use. On the other hand, it could reduce the pressure both on the commodity market and on the market for investment by recommending that the hours of labour should be reduced. It is only under such an organised system as we have outlined that a rational determination of these questions, which have previously been highly controversial political subjects, becomes possible.

As the productivity of labour increases there are three avenues through which the increase can be disposed of. Firstly, wages can be raised to increase consuming power and therefore expand the home market. Secondly, we can divert labour to the production of Capital goods—that is, equipping our factories with more modern plant, improving our transport system, rehousing the people, creating public buildings and improving the amenities of social life, and so on. Thirdly, we can *consume* the increased productivity in the form of increased leisure either by reducing the hours of labour or by increasing the number of holidays without reductions of wages.

We find it difficult, and often impossible, to do these things to-day because of the competitive struggle between producers either at home or abroad. Yet there are few who would deny that this is what ought progressively to occur as man's power over production increases. This argument has formerly been left to the Socialist. And it is the illogical and painful inability of the present system to utilise to the full the increased bounty of Nature and human invention which supplies the basis and indeed the partial justification for the Socialist attack on private enterprise.

I am here admitting the force of the argument, as every intelligent person must; but at the same time I am claiming to have advanced a set of proposals which would enable the social utilisation of wealth to be combined with the forms of industrial and commercial leadership to which we are accustomed. In the organised society we are discussing, this choice—as between increased consumption, capital extension, or increased leisure—would be made in accordance with the facts of the economic situation, and therefore for economic reasons rather than from emotional or idealistic impulse. In such a society the moral urge towards what seemed socially desirable would be regulated by the scientific determination of what was economically wise and possible.

Summary.—These questions which we have discussed under the heading of the functions of the Economic Council by no means exhaust the list of subjects which would come under review by that body. They are sufficient to convey, however, that such a body would perform an essential function by enabling industries jointly to discuss and settle problems in which they are mutually involved. They convey, also, the conception of the Economic Council as an adjunct to, rather than a substitute for, Parliament. It might be claimed that this form of economic organisation provides us with at least a possibility of achieving economic order without surrendering our political and social liberty.

I want now to devote some attention to an obvious criticism which may arise. It may be suggested that what has been advanced is a bureaucratic structure of organisation which would interfere with every impulse of private enterprise by regulation and restriction of every kind, and that in order to make the system work it would be necessary to control prices, profits, wages, salaries, rents, and every other charge now determined by the free play of competitive forces. The simple answer to this is that it is not true. In the next chapter

I shall endeavour to prove that, having eliminated anarchy from the market and from production, and having created an organisation through which Political and Financial policy will be directed towards the maintenance of stability, the separate industrial organisations can be left free to operate in response to the price indicator as they do at present. Too often Planning is made to look like a system of bureaucratic regulation. It is an essential difference between these proposals and any suggestion of bureaucracy that the Price Level could again become the universal guide, and that the economic system would operate again as an organisation in which private enterprise, working in a group system, would fulfil its necessary social function by conducting its commercial and industrial operations on profitable lines.

CHAPTER VI

ECONOMIC FREEDOM IN A SYSTEM OF ECONOMIC ORDER

THE title of this chapter has been put down in order plainly to contest the charge of Socialism and Bureaucracy which can always be made against proposals of this kind. In what has already been written a distinction has been kept clearly in mind between *licence* and *freedom*. It is not "freedom" which permits the anti-social aggressiveness of individual producers to wreck the market in a wild orgy of weak selling. It is not "freedom" which permits sectional interests in finance or commerce to seek their own profit at the risk of involving a whole community in ruin. This is licence. "Economic freedom" is that form of enterprise and initiative which operates within the limits of social responsibility. The vast majority of leaders in finance, commerce and industry are men who carry on their work regularly and consistently, regarding it as their particular job in life. They cannot fail to be familiar, however, with the financial "pirate" or the industrial "buccaneer" who makes his sudden swoop on to the field and strives to make his profit out of others' losses.[1] To check and restrain this "specula-

[1] Mr. F. Cresswell Pyman, managing director for Messrs. William Gray and Co., Ltd., Shipbuilders, speaking at the West Hartlepool Rotary Club, has illustrated the point. He said: "In days gone by, as depressions passed and good times returned there was nothing to stop any man who could snap up an old shipyard from building half-a-dozen ships, taking a

tive" irresponsibility is not the denial of freedom; it is the curbing of licence in order that others may be free.

The regulative powers with which the Industrial Councils would be entrusted would protect industry from this danger. The measures which would have to be taken by the representatives of finance to carry out their duties on the Economic Council would probably lead to the creation of a finance organisation which would check speculative disturbance in the field of finance and investment.[1] What we have to show in this chapter is that as a result of the forms of organisation proposed, the whole economic system could be entrusted to the direction of price as a guide to market conditions and the scale of production. We have already referred to the danger of monopolies exploiting the consumer through the high prices of scarcity. We have now reached the stage at which this possibility must be examined in greater detail. For if it is true

---

quick profit and clearing out. The door was open for unscrupulous exploitation of the industry and still worse for the workers."

[1] Report of the Macmillan Committee, para. 397 and 399.

". . . we believe that there is substance in the view that the British financial organisation concentrated in the City of London might with advantage be more closely co-ordinated with British industry, particularly large-scale industry, than is now the case."

"The functions which should be performed by such a concern may be summarised as follows:—Acting as financial advisers to existing industrial companies; advising in particular as to the provision of permanent capital, its amounts and types; securing the underwriting of and issuing the company's securities to the public, and, if necessary, assisting previously in arranging for the provision of temporary finance in anticipation of an issue; assisting in financing long contracts at home and abroad, or new developments of an existing company, or founding companies for entirely new enterprises; acting as intermediaries and financial advisers in the case of mergers or in the case of negotiations with corresponding international groups; and generally being free to carry out all types of financing business."

that the integrated industries for which we have provided would act in this way, then it would be impossible to leave prices to the free play of the market.

There are three separate angles from which this problem must be viewed. We referred in passing to the "efficiency" level of production. That is one aspect. The second is the "efficiency" level—or the level of maximum profitability—in marketing; and the third, which is really part of the second, the reaction of the consumer to price variations.

Let us look at each of these factors in turn.

The "efficiency" level of production is, briefly, that level at which the costs of production of any particular unit are lowest. A factory may be producing 250 pairs of boots, let us say, at a cost of 12*s.* per pair; by increasing its output to 500 the costs may fall to 10*s.* per pair. The manufacturers may experiment with another increase and find that, at a production level of 1,000, costs have fallen only to 9*s.* 6*d.* They may try increasing it to 2,000 and find costs do not fall below 9*s.* 6*d.* When they push production beyond the 2,000 mark costs may begin to rise again, because the expenditure needed for the handling of the greater quantity begins to exceed the economies of mass production. In that case the efficiency level of production would be from 1,000 to 2,000 pairs. This could be still further refined, possibly until it was found that a level round about 1,250 to 1,500 allowed a saving of another 3*d.* per pair.

The same kind of test can be applied to the factory or the unit of production whatever it may be. Mere bigness does not necessarily reduce production costs. There is an "efficiency" size for the factory or unit as well as an "efficiency" level of output when the size of the unit has been determined.

The level of maximum profitability in the marketing of goods is less easy to explain, for it is not subject to the same kind of precise determination. The reaction of the consumer to price variations differs according to the commodity concerned. If we were to take a commodity which he *must* have in order to live, and for which nothing could be substituted, then the consumer would be completely at the mercy of the organisation controlling the supply. But it is difficult to imagine a commodity of this kind unless it be a curative thing like radium or certain drugs—and these are already subject to a form of public control. Further up the scale we come to commodities to do without which would mean discomfort and hardship for the consumer. Here we find that the hardship can be mitigated by the use of substitutes. For instance, he might find it very inconvenient to do without bread, but if there was a plentiful supply of potatoes, other vegetables, fruit, etc., he could manage to get along with very little of it. Still further up the scale we come to commodities like cigars, gramophones, fur coats, and caviare, with which he could dispense altogether if the need arose.

The point of all this is that there is a limit beyond which the consumer cannot be forced in the attempt to rob him by high prices. This limit varies according to the choice open to him to purchase substitutes when the price of any article goes up too far. Every housewife is familiar with this. If eggs are too dear she will probably buy fish. If meat is too dear she will probably increase the number of cheese dishes in the family menu. In a word, there is a competition between different kinds of commodities which remains even after competition within any industry has been eliminated. Those who visualise monopolies as organisations able to hold a starving community to ransom are, therefore, over-stating their case.

But, of course, price is not determined by these "gangster" methods at all. The manufacturer supplying a commodity to the public endeavours to find the price at which he can sell that quantity which gives him the maximum return. If his boots have been selling at 35*s*. per pair he will have a certain level of sales showing a certain profit. By lowering the price to 25*s*. he may find he will double his sales and increase his profit. He may next find that by reducing the price to 20*s*. he can increase his sales again without reducing his profit and that below the 20*s*. level of prices his profit begins to disappear. As a result of this experimentation he will find that he can either supply a relatively smaller number of boots at 25*s*. or a greater number at 20*s*. and his rate of profit will remain the same. He may say, "Why should I have all the bother of selling more boots when I don't make any more money?" and confine his supply to the 25*s*. customers. But that is all he can do without injuring himself; that is the limit of his power to exploit the consumer.

It would appear, therefore, that among the factors operating to determine price in the new system of regulated production there will be one "constant" factor and two "variables." The "efficiency" level of production is called a "constant" factor because it is determined by purely scientific tests. It is a fact—there to be discovered. In the realm of marketing we find two variable factors which operate as follows. First, the response of the consumer to price variations will differ according to the choice open to him to select other commodities to satisfy his needs, and according to the importance of the need to be satisfied. Secondly, the most profitable level of marketing leaves the producer with a margin in which he is able, not so much to increase his profit as to indulge his laziness. And it may be remarked that against this indulgence the powerful interests of management and labour, as opposed to mere ownership, are continuously at work, since both these interests are naturally opposed to restriction of output.

These three factors must now be examined in relation to one another, for we cannot draw a distinction between the monopoly as a producer and the same monopoly as a seller. Any conflict which may be found to exist between its interests as a producer and its interests as a seller must be reconciled. And such a conflict may quite well arise. As a seller it may find that the maximum profit could be gained either by selling, let us say, 10,000 pairs of boots at 25*s.*, or 15,000 at 20*s.*; but as a producer it may find that the efficiency level of production would be 15,000 pairs. In that case it might find itself desirous as a seller to minimise its labours and take its profit at the lower level of production, but as a producer it would be conscious of the urge to maximise its sales in order to gain the production economies of the higher level of output. We must suppose that such an organisation would be seeking the maximum level of profitability both as a producer and a seller; and, therefore, in the circumstances just described, the limits within which it might exploit the consumer by the maintenance of scarcity would be still further reduced.

This question has been gone into in some detail because I anticipate that it is on this aspect of the proposals most of the criticism will fall. The examination does not prove that there is no possibility whatever of the monopoly exploiting the consumer in certain circumstances. It has shown, however, that very strict limits are placed upon its power to do so for the reasons which have been advanced. But it is not necessary to rely merely upon these arguments in order to show that the fear of any considerable exploitation is unfounded. In the earlier sections of this book we found that the whole system of trade rested upon the basis of the exchange of commodities against each other. In so far as any single monopoly was successful in maintaining unreasonably high prices (and we have seen that in the new economic organisation there would be very strict limits upon its power to do so) it would be scoring an advantage against the producers of other commodities. It would, in fact, be exchanging its boots for a greater number of hats, shirts, gramophones, railway journeys, etc., than they were really worth.

In the system we have visualised, however, not only would the producers of hats and gramophones themselves be organised as powerfully as the producers of boots; but they would be collectively organised in an Economic Council able to bring the force of public criticism to bear upon the anti-social acts of any one of its members. In considering this question, therefore, we have to remember that we are concerned not with the relationship between a single integrated industry and the consumers as a whole, but that the great mass of consumers will themselves be organised as producers in equally powerful bodies. In an earlier chapter reference was made to the fact that a single monopoly in an otherwise competitive society might be able to exploit the producers of its raw materials at the one end and the consumers of its finished products at the other. It must be obvious, however, that if the producers of its raw materials are equally as powerfully organised they will be able to resist any effort to exploit them by the offer of low uneconomic prices for their product.

It is equally true that in a society of organised industries any effort of a single industry to enrich itself by exploiting the consumer must be seen to be a blow at the stability of the market. By increasing its own claims on the purchasing power entering into effective demand it would be depleting the amount available for expenditure on other goods. The personnel of other industries would become concerned, therefore, not only as consumers, but as producers of other goods for which the market was declining. And, since purchasing power merely represents goods, an industry acting in the way we have suggested would really be forcing up the price of its own products by forcing down the price of the products of other industries.

We have seen the degree of protection against this danger which is afforded by market behaviour and considerations of the "efficiency" level of output. In so far as these checks might prove insufficient there is the additional check of the balance of power between one monopoly organisation and all the others. Moreover, there is the power residing in the Economic Council to recommend any necessary action to bring a recalcitrant industry to order.[1]

[1] Dealing with the same point in relation to Tariff policy in an article in the *News Letter*, May 28, 1932, the Rt. Hon. Walter Runciman said, "The Government, while recognising that it cannot itself undertake the reorganisation of industry or dictate the precise lines on which reorganisation should

In what has been said here we have been discussing the worst possible eventuality in a system of organised production, and crediting the monopoly concerns not only with the lowest possible motives, but with no sense of social responsibility at all. Now, it may be easy to imagine an individual being so keen on his own profit as to have no regard whatever for the welfare of his fellows, but it is difficult to imagine a large and responsible organisation controlled by a National Council behaving in this way. The very fact that they were entrusted with the responsibility of directing an important industry as a self-governing unit of our national life would bring from the great majority of people a response of willing co-operation. But even at the worst, imagining them to be interested in nothing but their own profit, we find that the market behaviour and the mass methods of production which we have been discussing provide adequate safeguards against any serious anti-social behaviour. When we add to these safeguards the restraining influence of equally powerful units of production in other fields and the power of the Economic Council to expose and con-

---

proceed, attaches the greatest importance to this aspect of national reconstruction. The Import Duties Advisory Committee are specifically charged under the Act with the duty of watching the interests of industries and trades which use goods on which additional duties are imposed, as well as those which produce them, and may at any time recommend the reduction or discontinuance of any of the additional duties. Further, the Board of Trade were given powers to collect compulsorily a large amount of information from protected industries which should enable a watch to be kept upon the effects of the new duties. The Government do not mean to allow the consumer to be exploited or the tariff to be used as a shelter for inefficiency. The simplest way to avoid these results would be to reduce or remove a duty. The Government have full powers to do this, and, if it becomes necessary, they will not hesitate to use it."

demn any action by one industry which would endanger the welfare of the others, it can safely be claimed that there is no ground whatever for alarm.

The importance of the point which all this argument has been advanced to establish cannot be over-estimated. It means that as a result of the integration of industries and the co-ordination of Economic and Political policy, we shall be able to preserve the price indicator as the guide in response to which the whole economic system will regulate and adjust itself automatically. If it is true that under the new system prices can safely be left to the free play of the market, then we have succeeded in constructing a new self-balancing economic system which will function without bureaucratic interference of any kind. It is submitted that this claim is justified and that the proposals of reconstruction here advanced on lines which aim at the preservation of self-government for industry are the only alternative to a policy of encroaching bureaucracy culminating in a situation in which all the functions of our economic life will have to be directed by the State.

If it is agreed that prosperity depends upon equilibrium between supply and demand, production and consumption, and savings and investment, then the maintenance of these equations must be the object of economic planning. There are only two ways in which that object can be served. If we fail to create a structure of industrial organisation which will enable industry to respond easily and intelligently to the price indicator, then we will be forced into the adoption of artificial devices such as quota regulation, price-fixing by Government Committees, Consumers' Councils, etc. If, on the other hand, industry is so organised that it is capable of intelligent anticipation and response to the market conditions indicated by prices, then these bureaucratic methods of regulation will be unnecessary. For this reason the policy of industrial reconstruction and co-ordination is seen to have an importance far greater than appears on the surface. It enables us to mark the limits of planning. The retention of the price system is the real dividing line between Socialist and non-Socialist ideas of planning. We are able to secure the benefits of order and equilibrium in our economic life without incurring the dangers of bureaucracy. Under present conditions it is not the price system which is at fault. Except in so far as prices may be artificially affected by monetary policy they merely record the condition of the market; they indicate scarcity or glut. It is, of course, essential to ensure that monetary policy will be devoted to the maintenance of stability and to the service of the industrial and commercial life of the nation. Provision is made for that in connection with the work of the Economic Council. The remaining fluctuation and dislocation arising from non-monetary causes must not be blamed on the price system. There is no simpler and better indicator that could be devised. It is clear, therefore, that our task is not to interfere with the price system itself, but to carry through the adjustments in organisation which will enable industry to respond intelligently to the market conditions it reveals.

But this is only possible if a *comprehensive* policy of re-adjustment and reconstruction is applied. We have already seen in practice that the partial effort leads to the creation of devices like price-fixing, quota regulation, rather futile efforts at coercion by *ad hoc* Committees, the setting up of Consumers' Councils, etc. It is true that the measures of planning which have already been applied have produced beneficial results for the industries concerned. But because these industries exist in an otherwise unplanned economy, these beneficial results can only be secured by the adoption of methods which threaten to produce a confusion of Committees and regulations in order either to make the plans effective or to protect the consumer from the abuse of the privileges which the State confers.

In the same way is it true that much of the propaganda in favour of planning creates the impression of bureaucratic organisation and control. These dangers and these suspicions arise from the fact that no one has yet thought out a general scheme of economic organisation into which each of these separate efforts or proposals will ultimately fit. Until and unless some conception of a new self-adjusting system is evolved, all planning proposals arouse the maximum of hostility because they appear to require a measure of State or bureaucratic regulation which would endanger the whole principle of self-government in industry. On the other hand, the proposals which I have outlined would enable industry to achieve self-government by giving it the power to fit itself for self-government. We escape the danger of bureaucracy, for, as has been shown, once the programme of organisational change had been carried out, the system would work as a self-balancing mechanism governed by the indicator of price.

There is, however, another criticism of these proposals to which it is not so easy to find a satisfactory answer. It is that the granting of monopoly powers to Industrial Councils may endanger the progressive application of new inventions and changes in the methods of production following upon the new discoveries in Scientific and Industrial research. At present there is opportunity and inducement for the entrepreneur to back his judgment by experimenting with new discoveries which may reduce production costs or improve the quality of commodities already on the market. It may be true that the profit incentive plays little or no part in influencing the Inventor or the Scientist. These are usually people completely absorbed in the work they are doing, and they would probably go on doing it whether the opportunities to exploit their discoveries for profit existed or not. Nevertheless, it is true that the widespread use of the new methods often depends upon the financial backing of the entrepreneur who sees the opportunity of profit by exploiting the new methods in competition with the old. If the Industrial Councils are to be granted monopoly powers in the production of their particular category of commodities, then the entrepreneur would not be free to set up redundant plant to produce a competitive article. In certain cases, of course, it would be to the advantage of the Industrial Council to adopt the new methods and no difficulty would arise; but it is useless to deny that there are circumstances in which the Industrial Council might prefer to go on using the older methods rather than incur the cost of re-equipping their industry in accordance with the new discovery.

Against this it may be urged that, so far as present experience shows, this danger has not materialised. The most highly integrated industries, such as the chemical industry, have in fact been the most progressive and intelligent users of modern scientific research. There would also be additional safeguards in the organisation as already described. Scientific and Industrial research workers would be represented on the Economic Council. No doubt they would be aware of the discoveries and inventions whose use was being blocked by any industry. They would be able to bring their information before the other members of the Economic Council and cause an inquiry to be made. The other industries who might be consumers or users of the product with regard to which the discovery or invention had been made would naturally be interested in action being taken to ensure that the full benefits of the new methods should be employed.

It is unlikely that any Industrial Council would lightly incur the charge of being guilty of the reactionary and anti-social behaviour in the suppression of inventions. The real difficulty arises not when the new method has proved itself to be superior, but in ensuring that it would be given a fair trial and the opportunities of experimentation. Experiences would probably furnish a method of escape from the difficulty. It may be that some extension and adaptation of the Department of Scientific and Industrial Research would provide a solution. Doubtless there will be other difficulties of this kind which cannot be anticipated; but, even so, the proposals advanced are not thereby invalidated. The problems and difficulties which would be encountered in carrying out this policy of industrial reconstruction can hardly be regarded as nearly so formidable as those which confront us to-day. We must not revert to the apathy of inaction because we cannot see clearly the solution of every problem which will arise; unless, of course, we can produce intelligent justification for the view that nothing need be done at all. That is a comfortable opinion most of us would be glad to accept. Unfortunately, all the evidence would seem to prove the need for action. We must, therefore, face the difficulties and deal with them as we can.

CHAPTER VII

FOREIGN TRADE

The essential feature of the proposals which have been advanced is that they are Protective. But "Protection" is seen to require something more than merely clapping on a Tariff. In our analysis we found that the stability of the market and the prosperity of industry and commerce were threatened in a variety of ways. The dangers of partial over-production; of disequilibrium in production; of a departure from the equation between Savings and Investment, and between production and consumption, have all been discussed, and a system of organisation proposed which would protect the market and the producer from the dislocation arising from these causes. We have found that this protection, and the stability which is so generally desired, can best be achieved not by attempting to plan and direct the whole economic system from the top, but by creating the conditions, and the necessary organisation, which will enable self-governing units of industry to achieve it for themselves. But the whole system which has been proposed has validity only if we are able to devise a method by which this national economy can be defended against the intrusion from abroad of all these dislocating factors through the channel of our foreign trade. There is still this gap in our armoury; and unless it can be repaired, everything which has been proposed must fall to the ground.

It has been estimated that in normal times one-third of British industrial and commercial activity is dependent upon foreign trade. We are dependent upon foreign sources of supply for a large proportion of our food supply and our supplies of the raw materials used by our manufacturing industries. We have to pay for these imports by the sale of a large volume of British products in overseas markets where they are subject to the competition of the products of all other countries. In the conduct of this foreign trade there are two ways in which the stability of our internal economy is endangered. The goods which we are importing from abroad enter into competition with similar goods produced at home. If they are sold at less than the costs of production in Britain the home producer suffers a diminution in his return, wages fall, unemployment is created, and this loss of purchasing power spreads the dislocation to other industries catering for the demands of the home market.

The goods we send abroad to pay for our imports have to be sold in competition, on the world markets, with the products of other countries. If the supply exceeds the demand, or if our competitors are content with a lower standard of life than we are, the prices will be low, wages and profits in British exporting industries are endangered, production is discouraged, unemployment is created, and again the consequent fall in purchasing power diminishes the home market.

To this statement of the case the Free Trader will reply that these evil results need not arise from the exchange of goods in competitive conditions on the world markets. He will hold that the sale of goods at low prices really increases the purchasing power of the consumers by enabling them to buy more goods for the same amount of money. Moreover, he will claim that there can be no difficulty in selling sufficient goods abroad to pay for our imports, because trade between countries is merely the exchange of goods and therefore payment for our imports must be taken by the rest of the world in the form of our exports of goods or services.

It would be impossible to do justice either to the complete Free Trade case or to the reply to it in a book of this kind, and our reply to this argument must therefore be brief. In the first place, even if it was admitted that this view would be correct if we lived in a completely Free Trade world, the fact would remain that we are not living in such a world, and we must deal with things as they are. In the second place, we have practical experience to show that the evil results have, in fact, occurred before our eyes in this country. The consequence of cheap imports has been reflected in the state of British agriculture. The consequences of low world prices for our exports is reflected in the state of Lancashire to-day. The fact is that the competition between countries in different stages of economic and social development tends to pull the advanced countries down to the level of their competitors. This is particularly true when the scope for outward market expansion is diminishing and the intensity of competition is consequently more acute. But, of course, to contest the need for some form of protection in order to raise and maintain the standard of life in Britain is to reject the whole view of the present economic situation on which this book is based. We must assume that the reader agrees broadly with the analysis which has been advanced. If so it will be obvious that the evils resulting from uneconomic prices either for imports or for exports must be dealt with if the new system is to function in such a way as to avoid lapses into depression at intervals of increasing frequency.

The object of any study of the methods by which our foreign trade might be regulated must be to maintain an equilibrium in the exchange of goods and services at the highest level rather than at the lowest. The effect of tariffs is to achieve a measure of protection for the home market without gaining for us, except to the modest degree in which tariff bargaining can be successful, any adequate protection for our exports. The quota system has had the effect, on the other hand, of achieving a measure of home market protection by assisting the foreign seller to charge higher prices to the British consumer than he would otherwise have done. It can at least be said in favour of the tariff method that the increased price paid by the consumer goes to the Exchequer in the form of customs revenue. Under the quota it goes to the foreign producer as additional and unnecessary profit. But the advocates of the quota system can claim that while it may be a more expensive method for the nation as a whole it is also more effective; and that, in the instances where it has been applied, it would have been difficult, if not impossible, rapidly enough to adjust a tariff in accordance with the sudden changes in price, to make it always effective as a protective instrument.

Another suggestion which has been advanced is for an Import Board which would purchase our main supplies in bulk; purchase the home supplies of the same commodity and average out the price to the consumer. This is open to the objection that it would mean the nationalisation of practically our whole system of distribution and, while it may be theoretically sound, it would encounter great opposition and difficulty in practice. Nevertheless, it is true that the tariff and quota systems cannot be regarded as adequate or sufficient for the maintenance of that stability which we have found to be so essential to economic welfare and prosperity. In recent years we have seen how Japanese competition is able to surmount tariff barriers as a result of the double competitive advantage of cheap labour and a depreciated currency. We are not at the end of that kind of competition in the world. Industrialism has already spread to the East. In a large number of commodities we can expect that the competition of Japanese labour will be followed by that of China [1] and other countries where labour is both plentiful and cheap. If it is reasonable to suppose that we will be faced in the future with an increasing competition of this kind—and it is difficult to see how this development can be prevented—then our economic structure must have more adequate protection than either a quota or a tariff will afford.

The proposals which have already been advanced in this book take us a step forward in the approach to a solution of this problem. The integrated industries

[1] The *Manchester Guardian*, 24th October, 1933, announces that Mr. Harold Briggs, of Oldham, has accepted an appointment as Technical Adviser to the Government of Canton for the building of cotton mills. Commenting upon his appointment, Mr. Briggs said, "No doubt the first object is to meet Japanese competition, but one can imagine what the effect may be upon Lancashire in the next ten years."

operating under their National Councils will, in the ordinary course of business, be seeking the advantages to be gained from the bulk purchase of their raw materials and the co-operative marketing of their finished products. The small-scale purchasing and selling by individual producers will give place to the expert buying and expert marketing of departments of the national industries working under the direction of the National Industrial Councils.

By the integration of industries into national units, therefore, we should already have travelled a considerable way towards reducing our foreign trade to some semblance of order. Each of the National Industries will, in any case, be engaging in bulk purchasing and co-operative marketing. It is suggested that it would be equally to their advantage and to the advantage of the nation as a whole if they were to carry out these operations in co-operation with one another, rather than as separate and unco-ordinated units. Representatives of the buying and selling organisations of each National Industry might be brought together to co-operate in the work of a national import and export Clearing House. It would then be within the power of such an organisation not only to gain the economies of bulk purchase but to use the bargaining power of this country, as the greatest market for food and raw materials in the world, to secure for our export trade some reasonable shelter from uneconomic competition in return for the custom we have to offer. It is not suggested that the method of bulk purchase should be applied to the whole range of our imports. The tariff would probably prove the most convenient method of dealing with a variety of articles of relatively small value which we might still be importing. But if the purchase of certain items of our food-stuffs, raw materials, and unmanufactured articles were brought under the co-ordinating control of a central Clearing House, our power to bargain for the exchange of goods and services in return for the imports we required would be very great indeed. This new possibility should be borne in mind in our search for a method by which stability could be maintained.

Everyone is familiar with the fact that our principal imports are food-stuffs and raw materials, and our principal exports manufactured goods.

The following table provides the classifications of our overseas trade in recent years:

OVERSEAS TRADE OF THE UNITED KINGDOM

(£ millions.)

	Total Imports.	Re-Exports.	Retained Imports.				Exports U.K. Produce and Manufactures.				Excess of Imports.
			Food, Drink and Tobacco.	Raw Materials.	Manufactures.	Total.	Food, Drink and Tobacco.	Raw Materials.	Manufactures.	Total.	
1924	1,277·4	140·0	541·2	323·8	266·0	1,137·4	57·0	106·5	618·9	801·0	336·4
1930	1,044·0	86·8	451·4	212·1	283·3	957·2	48·2	63·8	440·0	570·8	396·4
1931	861·3	63·9	396·6	147·3	244·3	797·4	35·5	47·0	292·0	390·6	406·8
1932	703·1	50·9	359·5	140·9	145·9	652·2	32·3	43·6	275·6	365·1	287·1

A detailed summary of the various items making up these three groups for the year 1932 will be found in Appendix A.

The twelve principal items of our retained Imports, and of our Exports of United Kingdom produce and Manufactures in the last three years and for 1924 were as follows:—

RETAINED IMPORTS

(£ millions.)

	1924.	1930.	1931.	1932.
Grain and Flour	118·3	71·1	54·8	56·8
Meat *	100·2	105·3	88·0	77·4
Butter and Cheese	61·2	58·2	53·3	48·9
Fresh Fruit and Vegetables	42·4	42·9	48·2	42·1
Wool and Timber	50·4	42·3	28·9	25·4
Raw Cotton	108·0	40·4	25·1	28·7
Sheep's and Lambs' Wool	39·1	25·8	21·8	20·6
Iron and Steel Manufactures thereof	22·0	23·0	19·5	8·6
Non-Ferrous Metals and Manufactures thereof	29·0	26·6	19·9	13·4
Textile Manufactures and Apparel	72·4	63·2	60·9	21·2
Chemicals and Oils †	17·9	15·9	15·5	11·7
Crude and Refined Petroleum	38·5	44·4	27·8	30·0

EXPORTS OF U.K. PRODUCE AND MANUFACTURES

(£ millions.)

	1924.	1930.	1931.	1932.
Beer and Spirits	12·86	9·22	7·30	5·84
Coal	72·1	45·7	34·7	31·6
Pottery, Glass, etc.	12·9	11·9	8·4	7·4
Iron and Steel and Manufactures thereof	74·2	51·3	30·4	28·0
Non-Ferrous Metals and Manufactures thereof	15·7	12·0	6·9	6·9
Electrical Goods and Apparatus	10·7	11·9	7·4	5·8
Machinery	44·8	47·0	33·0	29·5
Cotton Yarns and Manufactures	199·2	87·6	56·6	62·8
Woollen and Worsted Yarns and Manufactures	67·8	37·0	25·2	24·0
Silk and other Textiles and Apparel	59·8	40·9	27·9	26·0
Chemicals and Oils †	34·4	29·4	22·3	22·5
Vehicles (including Ships)	26·9	51·0	29·7	20·7

* Not including Poultry and Game.

† Trade Accounts—Class III. Groups N and O (Less Refined Petroleum in the case of Retained Imports).

For the year 1932 these twelve items of retained Imports account for £385 million out of a total of £652 million, or about 60 per cent. The twelve items of Exports of U.K. produce and manufactures represent £275 million out of a total of £365 million, or 75 per cent. It will be seen, therefore, that a large proportion

Countries.	Percentage of Total Imports.			Percentage of Total Exports.		
	1924.	1931.	1932.	1924.	1931.	1932.
BRITISH COUNTRIES.						
Self-Governing Dominions :—						
Irish Free State	4·00	4·24	3·77	5·90	7·81	7·06
Canada	5·16	3·81	6·14	3·50	5·26	4·49
Newfoundland	0·14	0·24	0·28	0·24	0·14	0·18
Australia	4·62	5·31	6·57	7·59	3·72	5·48
New Zealand	3·68	4·39	5·33	2·54	2·87	2·84
Union of South Africa	1·41	1·52	2·21	3·78	5·59	4·96
Total Self-Governing Dominions	19·01	19·51	24·30	23·55	25·39	25·01
India	6·17	4·26	4·60	11·31	8·27	9·34
Colonies, Possessions and Protectorates :—						
In Europe	0·27	0·41	0·56	0·71	1·27	1·53
West Africa	1·04	0·57	0·80	1·31	1·62	2·17
Rest of Africa	0·97	0·90	1·53	0·94	1·75	1·31
British Malaya	0·96	0·75	0·69	1·18	1·62	1·57
Ceylon	1·06	1·39	1·47	0·54	0·69	0·68
Hong Kong	0·06	0·05	0·04	1·07	1·13	1·32
Rest of Asia	0·15	0·24	0·33	0·21	0·39	0·58
West Indies, British Guiana, Honduras, etc.	0·49	0·59	0·95	0·80	1·46	1·72
Polynesia, etc.	0·03	0·06	0·15	0·05	0·10	0·10
Total Colonies, Possessions and Protectorates	5·03	4·96	6·52	6·81	10·03	10·98
Total British Countries	30·21	28·73	35·42	41·67	43·69	45·33
FOREIGN COUNTRIES.						
Soviet Union (Russia)	1·55	3·75	2·80	0·48	1·87	2·54
Succession States	2·48	3·09	3·38	1·40	1·21	1·53
Sweden	1·76	2·01	1·91	1·73	1·98	1·89
Norway	0·91	1·00	1·17	1·09	1·93	1·59
Denmark	3·83	5·42	5·77	1·72	2·22	2·70
Germany	2·89	7·45	4·32	5·32	4·71	3·99
Netherlands	3·34	4·09	3·13	3·15	3·51	3·32
Belgium	2·85	3·85	2·27	2·83	2·57	2·39
France	5·21	4·75	2·71	5·21	5·77	5·06
Switzerland	1·52	1·32	0·73	1·41	1·06	1·02
Spain	1·54	1·65	1·82	1·31	1·35	1·43
Italy	1·43	1·76	1·54	2·20	2·54	2·36
Rest of Europe	2·43	2·53	2·18	2·94	3·49	3·31
Egypt	3·00	1·26	1·48	1·89	1·70	1·79
Rest of Africa	1·04	0·80	0·75	1·85	2·19	2·27
Dutch East Indies	0·93	0·80	0·94	1·13	0·86	0·94
China	1·09	0·90	0·88	2·54	2·01	2·13
Japan	0·58	0·81	0·95	3·33	1·58	1·57
Rest of Asia	1·23	1·09	1·42	1·52	1·36	1·79
United States	18·88	12·07	11·90	6·74	4·67	4·14
Cuba	0·98	0·50	0·76	0·40	0·17	0·19
Brazil	0·38	0·66	0·59	1·70	1·04	1·28
Argentina	6·18	6·12	7·23	3·40	3·79	2·92
Chile	0·84	0·52	0·55	0·67	0·49	0·18
Rest of America	2·84	2·75	3·23	2·36	2·22	2·30
Polynesia, etc.	0·08	0·32	0·17	0·01	0·02	0·04
Total Foreign Countries	69·79	71·27	64·58	58·33	56·31	54·67
Total All Countries	100·00	100·00	100·00	100·00	100·00	100·00

of our trade falls into a relatively small number of categories. Consequently the effort to arrange a balance between purchases and sales is to that extent simplified.

The next thing we must look at is the sources of our supplies and the destinations of our Exports. The table on page 87, taken from the *Board of Trade Journal*, Feb. 16th, 1933, gives the percentage of total Imports received from, or Exports sent to, the various countries in 1924, 1931 and 1932.

The distribution between British and Foreign countries was as follows:—

Class of Trade.	1924.	1931.	1932.	1924.	1931.	1932.
	£'000.	£'000.	£'000.	Per cent.	Per cent.	Per cent.
Imports from :—						
British countries .	385,962	247,417	249,015	30·21	28·73	35·42
Foreign countries .	891,477	613,836	454,118	69·79	71·27	64·58
All countries . .	1,277,439	861,253	703,133	100·00	100·00	100·00
Exports (British Produce) to :—						
British countries .	333,769	170,673	165,532	41·67	43·69	45·33
Foreign countries .	467,198	219,949	199,606	58·33	56·31	54·67
All countries . .	800,967	390,622	365,138	100·00	100·00	100·00
Exports (Imported Merchandise) to :—						
British countries .	26,445	16,064	1,562	18·89	25·15	22·71
Foreign countries .	113,525	47,804	39,352	81·11	74·85	77·29
All countries . .	139,970	63,868	50,914	100·00	100·00	100·00

There was a considerable increase in 1932 in the British Empire proportion of our imports and exports. This, of course, results from the tariff preferences now granted by this country to Empire countries and from the agreements entered into at the Ottawa Conference. A survey of our trade since 1924 reveals a very marked increase in 1932 as compared with any of the earlier years in the proportion of our imports derived from the Empire. There has been a steep fall in our imports of manufactured goods from foreign countries and an increase in our imports of *other* goods from British countries. Although prices were still declining during

1932 and out total imports were reduced by £158 million, our imports from British countries increased by £1·6 million.

For our present purpose, however, it is necessary to summarise the situation in our overseas market as a whole. This can best be done by the inclusion of another table prepared by the Board of Trade showing the principal sources from which our imports were derived and the principal countries receiving our exports, in order of importance over a period of years.

Imports.

Country.	1932.	1931.	1930.	1924.
United States	1	1	1	1
Argentina	2	3	3	2
Australia	3	5	7	6
Canada	4	12	11	5
Denmark	5	4	4	8
New Zealand	6	7	8	9
India	7	8	5	3
Germany	8	2	2	12
Irish Free State	9	9	9	7
Netherlands	10	10	10	10
Soviet Union (Russia)	11	13	13	15
France	12	6	6	4
Percentage of total imports represented by imports from above countries	64·27	65·66	64·79	65·51

Exports.

Country	1932.	1931.	1930.	1924.
India	1	1	1	1
Irish Free State	2	2	2	4
Australia	3	9	3	2
France	4	3	4	6
Union of South Africa	5	4	8	7
Canada	6	5	5	8
United States	7	7	6	3
Germany	8	6	7	5
Netherlands	9	10	10	11
Argentina	10	8	9	9
Percentage of total domestic exports represented by exports to above countries	50·76	53·10	53·26	55·90

The purpose of this analysis has been to show that a relatively large proportion of our imports and exports is accounted for by a relatively small number of classes of goods, and that a considerable proportion of our total overseas trade, both imports and exports, is with a relatively small number of countries. Having established this fact and supplied the reader with the necessary figures to enable him to examine the question in greater detail for himself, it is now possible to return to the discussion of what system could be devised to safeguard the stability of the internal economic life of Britain while providing for the exchange of our products for the products of other countries.

The traditional attitude of mind in this country towards the problem of our foreign trade is very simple and direct. It is that "Exports must pay for Imports." To reverse the order of the sentence requires that we should reverse this attitude of mind. It arises, of course, from long association with the economic theories of Free Trade and from the dependence of this country on foreign sources of supply for its food-stuffs and raw materials. There are sound and solid reasons for an expansion of British agriculture, but they have little to do with an hysterical fear that we may find ourselves unable to purchase the means of life. Our need to buy food-stuffs from abroad is, to put it moderately, no greater than the need of foreign countries to sell them to us. Indeed, it is interesting to note that during 1931, in the worst period of the price slump, the average values (or prices) of imported food-stuffs and raw materials fell to a much lower level than the average values of our exports of manufactured goods. Taking the figure for 1930 as 100, the Board of

Trade index of average values for 1931 shows that Food, Drink and Tobacco imports fell to 81, Raw Materials imports to 73·5; while British exports of manufactured goods fell only to 89. This disparity has continued throughout the subsequent period, and we are now in the position of being able to buy the same *volume* of primary products with a much smaller volume of manufactured articles. The index figure for the whole of our imports for the year 1932 was 74·7, or 25·3 per cent. below 1930; while for the whole of our exports in 1932 the index of average values was 83·3, or 16·7 per cent. below 1930.

It is this attitude of mind, indicated by the phrase "exports must pay for imports," which leads to a fatalistic view of our trade relations with other countries. It results usually in an acceptance of the doctrine that we are quite helpless in the matter; that the British wage level, and therefore the expansion of the home market, cannot be determined by the productivity of British labour and capital resources; but that we must remain tied down to that standard of life which the prices obtained for our goods, in open competition with foreign labour, will permit. It is the purpose of this book, as indeed it has been the object of British policy since 1930, to contest and falsify this dogma.

It has already been stated that tariffs and quotas are inadequate for the purpose of safeguarding the equilibrium of our internal system from the dislocation of either "cheap" imports or "cheap" exports. The first step towards a solution lies in the integration, modernisation and reconstruction of British industry. The second step is to make the Import Duties Advisory Committee the nucleus round which could be built a new organisation for the regulation and control of our foreign trade. The purchasing and marketing sections of each of the national industries under the control of the National Industrial Councils could be brought together to assist and, for the purposes of foreign trade, to make use of an import and export Clearing House. This Clearing House would not require to make purchases and sales on its own account. Its purpose would be to co-ordinate and direct the purchases and sales of the other organisations which existed for that purpose. Such an organisation would at least enable us to pursue a conscious policy in our trade relations with other countries. It would allow our trade policy to be directed and controlled in accordance with the general economic policy which was being pursued by the nation as a whole, and give Britain freedom to determine her own future rather than let herself be dragged into a mad scramble of competition for markets with countries exploiting cheap labour in other parts of the world. We have now to see what policy it might pursue to give us the kind of "protection" we desire.

By means of this machinery the Economic Council would pursue three clearly defined aims:—

(1) To protect the home market from the dislocation of cheap imports.
(2) To maintain a balance in our foreign trade.
(3) To protect our export industries, and through them our whole internal economic structure, from the dislocation consequent upon their being forced to sell goods abroad at low prices.

The first and second points present no great technical difficulty. Complete protection of the home market could be secured by a combination of bulk purchase and, for miscellaneous imports, the tariff method. However low the prices paid for imports by the purchasing organisations might be, the level at which they were sold on the home market would be within our own power to determine. In this way the interests of the home producer of competitive goods could be safeguarded.

The maintenance of the desired balance between imports and exports would be achieved both by the quantitative and the tariff regulation of imports in accordance with anticipated market opportunities for our exports.[1] In this connection the question arises of the relative price levels between this country and the rest of the world. This will be referred to at a later stage.

The real difficulty is in connection with the third objective, and it is in order to secure this price protection for our exports that a new method of organising our foreign trade is mainly necessary.

[1] In the effort to maintain a balance in our foreign trade the "invisible" items in the balance sheet of our international transactions would, of course, have to be taken into account. These items include our income from Shipping, Overseas investments, and Commissions, etc. Our total credit balance on the whole of our overseas transactions—including both the "visible" and "invisible" items—in the years prior to the crisis were as follows: 1927 £114 million; 1928 £137 million; 1929 £138 million; 1930 £39 million. There are a number of questions which require careful study in this connection; particularly that of the direction of British overseas investment. It has been said, for instance, in the Macmillan Committee Report, "that in some respects the City is more highly organised to provide capital to foreign countries than to British industry." It is not the purpose of this book, however, to discuss such a highly technical question. We must be content to assume that the Economic Council would enlist the co-operation of its Financial representatives in action to ensure both the wise direction of foreign lending, and the provision of adequate capital to British industry.

Arising out of what has already been said there are a number of things which would contribute towards the realisation of these aims, which might now conveniently be summarised.

(*a*) The integrated national industries would be conducting their operations on more economical and efficient lines. Their competitive efficiency would be greatly increased. The competition between British producers selling their goods abroad would be eliminated and the substitution of centralised and expert selling would produce a saving out of which more adequate representation of British goods in foreign markets could be financed. There are a number of items in our export trade, especially where superior technical skill and the factor of reliability come into play, in regard to which this improved production efficiency, the elimination of competition, and the superior selling methods would be sufficient to secure remunerative prices—and that even if the present conditions of open competition with the products of less advanced countries should continue.

(*b*) The mobilisation of our bargaining power as consumers with large orders to place in respect of goods (food and raw materials) for which we are the largest customers in the world, would place us in a powerful position to negotiate reasonable preference for our exports. The co-ordination of our purchases through the Clearing House would provide a greater power of flexibility in the selection of our sources of supply.

(*c*) The British self-governing Dominions already take 25 per cent. of our exports and supply 25 per cent. of our imports. The Crown Colonies and Possessions take 11 per cent. of our exports and supply $6\frac{1}{2}$ per cent. of our imports. India takes 9·34 per cent. of our exports and supplies 4·60 per cent. of our imports. These areas provide an important outlet for British capital investment. A wisely conceived Empire trade policy would extend the opportunities for new capital expansion and increase the flow of trade between countries in the British connection. A country with its trade organised on the lines proposed would be able to direct a policy of real Empire development by rescuing its trade from the haphazard direction of a multitude of individuals seeking only cheapness in their operations. We could provide Empire countries with a guaranteed market at remunerative prices in return for equal advantages in their markets. Our expenditure on the protection and development of the Crown Colonies entitle us to bring them into a closer relationship with the economic life of Britain. The open market policy should be abandoned and the prosperity of the Colonial areas sought by linking their economic life to that of Britain through the mutual adoption of reciprocal preferences, to ensure remunerative prices for goods exchanged in trade.

On this basis an Empire trade policy could be built which would attract the Dominions into an increasing closer co-operation with the general economic policy of this country.

(*d*) In the list of countries quoted on p. 89 supplying 64 per cent. of our imports and taking over 50 per cent. of our exports, it will be seen that the United States and Argentina occupy first and second place in order of importance as importers into Britain. On the list of countries receiving our exports, however, the United States comes seventh and Argentina tenth. The use of our bargaining power in these and other cases ought to secure more favourable conditions for British exports. It must be remembered that we should not be seeking imports *at low prices* so much as economic prices for our exports. In so far as these countries were also desirous of pursuing a stable price and high wage policy their price level would be in greater conformity with our own. It is possible indeed that so far as the United States is concerned they might be prepared to enter into arrangements with regard to both monetary and trade policy which would enable a high wage area in the world to secure mutual protection from the market depredations of nations on a lower standard of life.

By the full utilisation of all these powers and possibilities our overseas trade organisation might be enabled to solve its problem. In so far as these methods were found to be insufficient, we should be left with a margin of foreign trade in regard to which the prices obtained for our exports would not be sufficient to maintain the standard of life in the industries concerned at a level which would permit the home market to expand. In that case we should be in the position of having to choose between two alternative policies. First, we could scale down our export industries; and at the same time expand agricultural and other industrial production to take the place of imports.

We could thus reduce the volume of our imports to the level at which exports at remunerative prices could be maintained. Such an adjustment, if forced upon us in this way, would naturally reduce the advantages which a high level of foreign trade secures in the division of labour between countries, according to their climate and resources. But it is not an impossible adjustment to make, and if only a small proportion of our foreign trade was left unprotected, would not prove unduly inconvenient.

The alternative course would be to pay to the producers in the export industries a deficiency price to make up their returns to a level which equalled their production costs. The one thing which could not be tolerated would be to allow production to be discouraged, unemployment to be created, or the purchasing power of the workers to be diminished. If that happened, then we should be back to the old conditions in which depression is allowed to attack the home market through a section of industry being exposed to the menace of low prices.

The deficiency payment is, of course, a subsidy. It may be objected to on that account; but it must surely be evident that the payment of a subsidy would be preferable to the abandonment of any effort to protect the system from the results of low prices which would spread throughout the whole structure of industry and commerce.

There are two ways in which such a payment could be made. It could be paid direct from the Exchequer from money raised by the ordinary methods of taxation, thus spreading the burden over the nation as a whole. Or it could be paid by the overseas trade organisation out of profits made on the purchase of imports at low prices and their sale in the home market at a higher level. The second method would enable the critics to raise the cry of dear food, yet it would be a fair method in the circumstances which would exist.

The fact that a section of our export trade was left unprotected in this way could only mean that remunerative trading arrangements had not been possible over a wide enough area. To exactly the same degree, therefore, as we had to bear the handicap of low prices for our exports, we should be enjoying an advantage in cheap imports. The low prices for our exports would be balanced by low prices for our imports. It will be obvious that if the whole of trade was being conducted by a single individual, the actual money terms in which the value of the goods being exchanged was expressed would not matter. He would be receiving an adequate volume of the goods he wanted to buy in return for the goods he wanted to sell. But when the exchange takes place between large numbers of individuals at different prices for different goods the receipt of low prices does matter.

The low return in money might buy an adequate quantity of *some* goods but an inadequate quantity of others. The producer receiving the low prices would suffer a loss unless the prices of all the goods he purchased for consumption fell to the same extent as the price he received for the goods he sold. This loss, as we have seen, would reduce his power to buy, discourage his employment of labour, and in time spread dislocation to other industries until the process of adjustment of all prices to the lower level had been completed. This is really the familiar difficulty of the sheltered and unsheltered trades. The argument for the payment of a deficiency price by the overseas trade organisation out of profits levied upon the cheap imports rests upon the view that not to do so would mean that all the consumers would, in these circumstances, be profiting temporarily out of the losses of the unlucky exporter. But it is comparatively unimportant who pays the deficiency price so long as it is paid. If the nation finds it necessary to maintain production in any industry at unremunerative prices in order to balance its foreign trade account, this burden must be equally spread over the more profitable forms of production or disequilibrium in prices will lead to depression during the difficult process of adjustment. But, although we have examined these two courses separately, it is more likely that in practice a solution of the difficulty would be sought by a combination of both methods. If a particular industry was faced by a *temporary* collapse of prices in its export markets, then a deficiency payment in order to nurse the industry past the danger point of crisis would be the obvious and common-sense course to adopt. But if a considerable margin of our export trade was threatened with the danger of being left unprotected *permanently*, then it would be necessary to scale down its production for export; expand the home production of goods which we formerly imported in exchange for these exports; and, in the intervening period of adjustment, give temporary assistance to the industry to maintain the employment and the purchasing power of its personnel.

Adjustments of this kind will have to be carried out by the Economic Council in any case. Indeed, it is a process from which there is no escape. Well-informed leaders in the Coal-mining, Cotton Textile, and Shipbuilding industries have repeatedly stated that it is useless to expect these industries, in the conditions of the modern world, to regain the supremacy and employing capacity they formerly enjoyed. Unless we are to be content to carry the displaced workers in idleness, as a permanent charge upon the nation, employment must be provided for them elsewhere. It was in anticipation of this problem that the statement was made in Chapter II that: "Having sought the highest possible level of stable commercial relations with other countries, our task is then clearly one of adapting our internal production to a new equilibrium in which the supply of goods and services will equal demand, and, *because of correctness in proportion*, exchange freely on the home market."

Or, to put it in another way, we must provide for an increase in the exchange of goods between our own nationals, to compensate for any decline in the opportunities to conduct the exchange of goods with the nationals of other countries. But, even if we are not compelled of necessity to carry through these adjustments, it is obviously desirable that in so far as it is possible a planning authority would seek to expand our markets for the more highly skilled products where the rewards are greater for the same expenditure of labour. These are the kind of adjustments for which it will be the function of the Economic Council to provide. Moreover, in the development of new industries or the expansion of old ones account would have to be taken of the distribution of our population and of existing social capital, such as housing accommodation, transport facilities, water, electricity and gas services; schools; public buildings and the like.

Confronted with the limitations upon the expansion of foreign trade on a fair basis of exchange, a nation organised to surmount its difficulties would turn to the more intensive exploitation of its own resources to provide employment for its people and to maintain its standard of life.

Some reference must be made to the effects of monetary policy upon the conduct of foreign trade. It is very probable that the adoption of the policy which had been advocated here would mean that the British price level would be higher than that of other countries —especially the new industrial countries with a cheap and plentiful labour supply. In the absence of a trade organisation of the kind proposed, what would normally happen is that the exchange value of sterling would fall—or, if we were under an International Gold Standard, gold would be withdrawn. This process is very clearly summarised in an interesting document[1] issued by the London Chamber of Commerce in 1932 which deserves the attention of all serious students of the question.

> *Price level.* It is generally assumed that the International Gold Standard system provided an automatic currency. It did, in the sense that currency was taken from a country automatically whenever some foreign nation, whether for political reasons or otherwise, withdrew gold, but it was certainly not automatic in relation to the

[1] "Monetary Policy." Report by a Special Committee of the London Chamber of Commerce. A supplement to the Chamber of Commerce Journal, July 1932.

needs of producers and consumers within the country.

Let us take the position of the manufacturer under the International Gold Standard system, who, having sold 100,000 units in one year and seen his sales steadily rising as time goes on, decided that he can, in the next year, dispose of 150,000. He enlarges his plant accordingly, and starts to manufacture at that rate. For some political or other reason, quite remote from the needs of producers and consumers, France, or some other country, withdraws gold, currency is contracted, prices fall, and the manufacturer has his product left on his hands, or he must sell it at a loss. Alternatively gold flows in, prices rise, and the manufacturer shows an abnormal profit. This encourages the formation of new companies to manufacture the same article, seeing so large a profit is to be earned by so doing. Gold is once more withdrawn, prices fall, and those new companies are ruined, probably dragging the original company with them.

It is submitted that a monetary system which ensures equilibrium amongst nations by such methods is out of date in a scientific age.

In theory, if prices generally are higher in country A than in country B, country A is a good country for B to sell in, but a bad one for it to buy from. Instead, therefore, of taking out the payment due to it for its sales, in the form of goods, country B takes them out in the form of gold. The loss of gold suffered by country A should induce it to contract its currency and credit, with the result that its prices would fall. Country B, on the other hand, having acquired additional gold should expand its currency, with the result that prices would rise, thus once more restoring equilibrium to the balance of payments between the two countries.

The reaction in country A, in times past, to this crude method of control, was that wages were promptly lowered, and strenuous efforts were thereupon made by manufacturers to increase their export trade in order to compensate for the reduced internal purchasing power. If this failed, unemployment necessarily followed. Moreover, the influx of the fresh gold into country B usually had the effect of raising country B's prices and making it less competitive, so that country A was soon in a position to regain some part of, if not all, its lost gold.

We have been assuming that as a result of the co-ordination of Industry, Finance and Politics on the Economic Council, monetary policy would be made subservient to the needs of productive industry and of national economic prosperity. At some stage in the future, however, a return to the Gold Standard may be considered possible and desirable. It is the most convenient method for the preservation of confidence and the adjustment of small discrepancies in the balance of payments between countries. If, however, it were to involve the crude methods of adjustment described by the London Chamber of Commerce, then it is unlikely that it would be tolerated for long by a country which has already suffered so much from the same cause. But if a return to the Gold Standard was accompanied by the adoption of the control of foreign trade which has just been advocated, then these dangers would cease to exist. The flow of gold to adjust international balances could be kept within limits by exerting a control over our balance of imports and exports of goods and services. Monetary policy could thus be kept comparatively free from preoccupation with the preservation of gold stocks or the maintenance of exchange rates. We should be able to regulate our trade in such a way as to avoid a discrepancy in the balance of payments of such dimensions as to require adjustments in monetary policy which would endanger internal prosperity in order to preserve the external stability of sterling.

It is submitted that the organisation which has been described would provide a complete safeguard against whatever price or currency fluctuations in the rest of the world might endanger the stability of the home market and the prosperity of home producers. The raw materials purchased from abroad would be supplied direct to the national industries at the price at which they were purchased plus any administrative charges incurred, provided they were not materials which were in competition with any form of home production. In the case of food-stuffs or other bulk imports which were being produced at home, the marketing would be done through the ordinary trade channels at prices and in quantities which safeguarded the interests of the home producer.

Through this co-ordination of our purchases from, and our sales to, other countries, we should be able to maintain a correct balance between our imports and exports. Our internal production would be freed completely from the dislocation arising from the currency and tariff fluctuations in the rest of the world. At the same time we should be able to keep our trade with other countries at the maximum level suitable to our internal requirements, for we should be assured of a volume of sales to equal our volume of purchases. We should not be in the position of pursuing a policy of narrow economic nationalism. On the contrary, we should be making a considerable contribution towards a return to such stable international conditions of trade as would tend to lessen the friction between nations. We should be setting an example of the method by which the exchange of goods between countries might be conducted to their mutual advantage in the changed circumstances of the modern world.

This brief indication of the methods by which our foreign trade might be regulated arises naturally from the form of organisation which has been proposed for our national industries. It raises the question, however, whether it is proposed to organise the distribution of goods to the consumer on the same lines. There are many arguments which could be advanced in favour of such a course. The present methods of competitive distribution are undoubtedly wasteful in that there is a great duplication of effort in the performance of the same function. As a result of industrial integration it follows that the National Councils for Industry would be in a position to ensure a more orderly *wholesale* distribution of their products. The marketing of a large proportion of our food supplies is already being regulated under the Agricultural Marketing Act. A more efficient system of distribution is required, however, for the other commodities which fall outside these categories and some form of contact between wholesale distribution and the Economic Council would be desirable. A suitable organisation for this purpose may be the British Distribution Committee[1] now being formed. With the assistance of some such body internal market requirements could be studied and a supervisory distributive organisation created through whom imported supplies would reach the ordinary channels of wholesale and retail trade.

This form of organisation for the regulation of our foreign trade is proposed not because the writer has any predisposition in its favour. But the experience of the past two years has shown clearly that a much more efficient method than the tariff or the quota is necessary. It is not a simple problem of protecting the home

[1] In a letter to *The Times*, Oct. 20th, 1933, a provisional committee of this organisation states:—

"Between every producer of consumer goods and his ultimate market lies this vast distributive machine of the wholesale and retail trades. The producer must use this machine to transfer his goods to the consuming public; the public must use the same machine to satisfy their wants.

"How deplorable it is, then, that our knowledge of the structure of distribution, its operating costs, and the markets it serves should be so remarkably slight.

"These circumstances clearly demand, and demand urgently, the formation of a British Distribution Committee. The task of this body will be the collation of existing data bearing on distribution, the co-ordination of efforts for improving such data, the promotion in due course of a census of distribution, and generally the improvement of distributive methods and technique."

This letter was signed by the following:—

LORD LUKE, Chairman, British National Committee, International Chamber of Commerce.
PAUL S. CADBURY, Cadbury Brothers, Limited.
JOHN CLARK, Chairman, J. and P. Coats, Limited.
J. E. JAMES, Secretary, Imperial Chemical Industries, Limited.
F. J. MARQUIS, Lewis's, Limited.
McDOUGALLS, Limited.
HAROLD MACKINTOSH, John Mackintosh and Sons, Limited.
ALEXANDER GRANT, Chairman, McVitie and Price.
F. D'ARCY COOPER, Unilever and Lever Brothers, Limited.

market which confronts us—although even in that respect the present methods can hardly be called satisfactory—but the protection of the home market while at the same time maintaining the level of our foreign trade. The mere balancing of imports and exports is not sufficient. We require a method by which the balance can be achieved and maintained at a high rather than a low level. By that test the tariff and quota methods are seen to be inadequate. It is submitted that the method here advanced would be both practicable and effective.

This description of the new technique for the regulation of foreign trade completes the structure by which it is claimed that prosperity and stability could be achieved. The Industrial Councils, the Import and Export organisation and the Economic Council constitute together a form of organised direction and control which would at least provide the machinery through which an economic policy could be made effective. Not only would it enable production to be related to supply, but the balance of power on the Economic Council would enable a proper restraint to be maintained over the price policy of the industries. Moreover, in such an organised economy the mutual dependence of industry would surely be self-evident. The producers in one industry would be seen to be the customers for the products of the others. Not only would equilibrium between productive capacity and market demand be maintained for each industry separately, but it would have then become possible to maintain an equilibrium in the quantities of each product which would enable exchange to take place on the home market at the highest level of general productivity. The balance would be achieved and maintained by a scientific direction of new capital investment. The balance between Saving and Spending and between Saving and Investment would for the first time be made amenable to intelligent conscious direction, and the standard of life be permitted to rise, both by increased material wealth and increased leisure, to equal the advance in productivity due to Science and Invention.

CHAPTER VIII

LABOUR

In the foregoing chapters the whole question of the position of labour in this new structure of economic organisation has been deliberately ignored. This has not been because of any under-estimation of the importance of the question, but because it could not be dealt with until a clear impression had been conveyed of the kind of social and economic circumstances to which any labour policy would have to be related. The material relations between labour and management to-day are largely conditioned by the fact that they are each the victims of circumstances they cannot control. In this sphere, the struggles, disputes and disagreements arise with regard to the division of the products of industry—the sharing of the rewards of effort. So far we have concentrated upon the presentation of a case for such a reorganisation of our industrial life as would at least ensure the continued existence and, we hope, increase the total volume of the benefits, or rewards, to be shared.

In presenting this case we have seen that many of the questions which were formerly settled by the haphazard conditions of the market, or by individual reaction to the circumstances of the time, must in future be brought within the control of an authority which would endeavour to master economic events rather than be mastered by them. This structure has been devised in order to achieve a direction of the economic destinies of the nation and change the circumstances in which industry and commerce have to be conducted. It cannot, therefore, be regarded as powerless to affect the disputes between labour and management arising from the disorderly conditions which it is designed to abolish. The possibilities of reconciling the conflict of interest between workers and their employers will have been enormously increased as a result of bringing under intelligent control the conditions from which, at present, the conflicts arise.

In regard to each of the questions which we have already discussed—the protection of the home market from cheap imports, the low prices of uneconomic competition and weak selling, or a failure of investment to equal savings—we have seen the importance of defending the market from the effects of a loss of purchasing power and the consequent failure of effective demand. The object of our whole scheme of organisation is to provide for the maintenance of the various equations on which the prosperity of industry depends. It must be obvious, therefore, that in determining the rewards of labour the same principles must apply. If the standard of life of the worker is not maintained, the whole system of balance between production and demand will be destroyed. It is true that it would be possible to restrict production and keep the worker poor, but in the new conditions there would be no benefit to anyone in such a policy. The aim of the Economic Council would obviously be to maintain an equilibrium between supply and demand by the expansion of demand rather than by the restriction of supply. The reward of labour, therefore, ceases to be a detail to be settled by the relative power of rival organisations of workers and employers, and becomes a significant and important aspect of general economic policy.

Immediately this point is grasped it is seen that an entirely new consideration is introduced into the determination of wage rates. For the worker must now be regarded as economically important not only as a producer but as a consumer as well. In a society which makes any attempt to plan the maintenance of equilibrium, the determination of the worker's standard of life ceases to be merely a private matter between him and his employer and becomes a matter of importance to all other industries dependent for their prosperity upon the ability of the worker to buy the goods and services which they supply.

But there is another important aspect of the question which must be examined as a preface to our consideration of the main problem. In discussing the price policies which might be pursued by monopolies it was stated that if one industry managed to force up the price of its products beyond the proper level, it would, in fact, be increasing its own rewards by reducing the rewards of other industries. If it is kept clearly in mind that money merely represents goods and services, then it is obvious that a rise in the price of boots, for instance, means that they will be made to exchange for a greater number of hats, gloves, or railway journeys than they are really worth. The effect of this is to increase the exchange value of boots and reduce the exchange value of hats, gloves, etc. The rewards of the boot industry increase and the rewards of the hat industry are reduced.

This same argument can now be applied to labour. In the economy we are visualising it is anticipated, for reasons which were stated in Chapter VI, that commodities would exchange at approximately their fair costs of production. It follows, therefore, that labour costs will play a considerable part in the determination of prices. Now, if the workers in one industry managed to force up their wages to an exceptionally high level, the cost of production and, therefore, the price of their product, would also rise. The effect of this would be that the price of other commodities in terms of goods would be correspondingly lowered and the incomes of workers in other industries would buy less. It will be seen, therefore, that just as we found it necessary to make provision, in the Economic Council, for what might be called a second line of defence for the consumer against an injurious price policy, so must we provide for a check on wage policies in the light of broad social considerations. The wages of any section of workers must not be allowed to fall in such a way as to injure market stability, nor must they be allowed to rise so high as to inflict injury on the standard of life of other sections of workers, as consumers. It is not suggested that wages can or should be equal in all industries, but it is suggested that a system of wage negotiation should be devised which will enable us to ensure that they are equitable.

One result of the change in industrial organisation which has been proposed would probably be that Trade Unions would tend to adjust their groupings on similar lines to the management side of industry—that is to say, the present tendency of Craft Unionism to give place to Industrial Unionism would be accelerated. It is suggested that under the new system the Trade Unions should be encouraged to promote this development and to produce a structure of organisation which will correspond to the structure of industrial management which has been advocated. The workers in each industry should be organised on the same lines as the industry itself. A workers' national Trade Union Council should be formed to correspond with the National Council responsible for the conduct of each industry. In each district or functional grouping of an industry for management purposes there should be a corresponding grouping of workers in their appropriate Trade Unions. At every point from the workshop or factory to the National Council there would then be a body representing management and a body representing the workers.

Management.	Labour.
National Council for the Industry.	Trade Union representative National Council of Workers in the Industry.
Functional Subdivisions of Management within the Industry.	Functional groups of Workers' representatives.
Area or District units on the Management side.	Trade Union area or District Committee.
Works organisation.	Trade Union Works Committee.

The formation of this parallel structure could not, of course, be brought about compulsorily, but it would naturally follow from the recognition of the Unions and from the request that a body entitled to negotiate on behalf of all classes of workers in the industry should be available for consultation by each district or functional group and each National Industrial Council.

A co-ordinating body of workers' representatives, corresponding to the Central Economic Council, should also be formed. Until the necessary adjustments in Trade Union organisation had taken place, the Trades Union Congress General Council might be regarded as the organisation with which the Economic Council would be able to deal. We would thus have a duplicate structure throughout the whole field of economic activity.

Conciliation machinery for the settlement of disputes would be created at each point. The district or functional groups of management and labour would deal with any friction which might arise with regard to workshop conditions or the general details regarding the conditions of labour. The National Councils of management and labour would deal with wages, hours of employment, and such larger questions for the industry as a whole. The full terms of all agreements with regard to wages and hours of labour in each industry would be submitted to the Economic Council to be registered and approved. In the event of labour and management in any industry failing to reach agreement, the dispute would be submitted to the Economic Council for inquiry and recommendation. Until this inquiry had been held and the Economic Council's recommendations published, no interruption of employment would be permitted either by the declaration of a strike or a lock-out. The decision or recommendation of the Economic Council would not be binding on the parties to the dispute. The right of the worker to withdraw his labour would not be infringed. The right of the management to terminate the employment of their workers would not be interfered with.

This preservation of the freedom of both labour and management to resort, in the end, to action which would close down the industry may appear to be a weakness in a policy which is designed with the object of maintaining stability by protecting the market and the producer from anything that may threaten the equilibrium of production and demand, of prices and costs, or of savings and investment. Why, it may be asked, should this loophole be left to endanger the whole economic life of the nation? The answer is that it could only be closed by resorting to compulsory arbitration, and compulsory arbitration belongs to the rigid doctrines of dictatorship. It would be easy to construct a system which, on paper, would be completely water-tight and logical. But we are dealing with human beings; and it would be found, in practice, that the effort to coerce either employers or workers in matters of this kind would lead to resentment and revolt. This, in turn, would lead to more coercion, until in the end the nation was stripped completely of the individual and civil liberties which we desire to preserve. Socialism or Fascism may adopt these methods of coercion, but the whole purpose of this book has been to advocate an alternative to these sterile cults which, by their blind worship of mechanical efficiency, would rob the nation and the individual of every right of self-expression and cultural freedom.

But is the danger really so acute? It must be remembered that the negotiations would not be taking place under the pressure of the low prices of uneconomic competition. The market would be stable; prices would be at a profitable level, and the industry would be free to devote its attention to the economies of efficiency. The fact is that the real dispute could not arise between the workers and employers in a particular industry at all. The higher wages, if granted, would be, in the eyes of the Economic Council, a justification for higher prices if it could be shown that the previous level of prices would now be unprofitable.

The real dispute would be between a section of the workers and the Economic Council itself. In effect that would mean a dispute between the workers in one industry against the combined opinion of industry as a whole. If there was justice in the workers' case, there could be no inducement for the Economic Council to resist it. If there was no justice in it, the responsible leaders of labour would hardly be so unwise as to oppose the united will of a body concerned only with the preservation of conditions which would serve the interests of industry as a whole.

The Economic Council could have no interest in keeping the standard of life of the worker at a low level. To perform its function of preserving equilibrium it would, on the contrary, be concerned to expand the market as the productive power of industry increased. The only circumstances in which a dispute of this kind could arise would be if a section of workers were advancing demands which could only be met by sacrificing other workers in other industries. Such a contingency is not likely to arise. The Economic Council would merely be discharging an important economic function in regard to wage demands of preserving the balance between the claims of one section of the nation and another. In doing that it would be more likely to secure the co-operation than to incur the enmity of labour.

There is, however, another aspect of the question of the position of the worker in this new society which must be dealt with here. There is the claim of the Trade Unions for a share in the management and control of industry. This claim is not advanced because of any illusion that the workers have more skill and ability in the technique of management than the owners or the salaried staff now charged with that responsibility. It is a claim which is often associated with the policy of Nationalisation, and its object is to ensure that the welfare of the workers will receive first consideration. But even in connection with the policy of Nationalisation there have been recent indications of a change of view as trade union and labour leaders emerge from the clouds of propaganda and face the practical questions of the day. The old demand for State ownership and workers' control seems to be giving place to a demand for public utility ownership and independent control. The more clear-sighted leaders have already recognised that ownership is of less importance than management, and that the idea of management being representative must be abandoned in favour of its being independent and efficient. The fact is, of course, that the ordinary worker is not particularly interested in theoretical formulas regarding his vicarious representation in discussions of technical problems. He is interested to ensure that his wages, hours and conditions of labour will be improved and that the general policy of the industry should be directed towards the maintenance of his standard of life and the abolition of poverty and insecurity.

These desires are shared by a great many people who reject the doctrinaire Socialism with which the simple demands of the worker are so often unjustifiably associated. Most people will agree that as the power to produce is increased, the standard of life should rise; that the conditions of large sections of the working population to-day is a measure of the failure of "Free Capitalism"; and that our processes of production and distribution ought to be so rationalised as to abolish undeserved poverty and insecurity from the life of the nation. The demands of the workers as a class are justified by the abundant possibilities with which science and invention have endowed us. But the acceptance of this view does not require our surrender to the barren doctrine of bureaucratic organisation and control.

In so far as the demand is not merely political propaganda, it represents a legitimate claim that as the worker's welfare is bound up with the prosperity of industry, he is entitled to some voice in the determination of the general policy it pursues. In the new structure of economic organisation the detailed questions regarding the general conditions of labour will be well enough safeguarded by the provision of facilities for consultation between management and labour. The general policy questions in which it is claimed the voice of labour should be heard will be dealt with by the Economic Council. Interference in the daily management of industry must clearly be rejected. Those entrusted with that highly technical task should be chosen for their ability. On the other hand, representation of labour on the Economic Council should be conceded not only because it is just but because it would be helpful to the work of the Council. We would then be provided with a real possibility of co-operation. The two parallel structures, of management and labour organisation, would carry out the necessary negotiations within the industries on all minor questions, and be brought into unity on the Economic Council for the discussion of the general questions of economic policy. On this body the representatives of labour would find their opportunity not only of looking after the interests of the workers as a whole, but of serving these interests by making their contribution towards the progress and advancement of a system of co-operative effort.

So far we have only been describing the mechanics of the system. It must not be imagined, however, that the relationship between labour and management as here defined is regarded by the writer as either ideal or final. These proposals are being advanced as immediately possible of application, and both suggestion and comment have had to be limited in close relation to the facts of the present situation. One of these facts is the mood of antagonism which exists between sections and classes in the community. But if it is reasonable to hope that the new system in operation will produce a new spirit and that the antagonism will die as the basic factors causing it are removed, then we might anticipate a time when the organisations of labour, management, and ownership will grow out of this attitude of hostility and become fused in a spirit of co-operation and common effort.

If the instability and fluctuation which now gives rise to friction is removed, this hope might easily be fulfilled. And such a development is important, for there is much more involved in the problem which we are discussing than the material question of wages. A great part of the malaise and discontent among the workers is due, not merely to dissatisfaction with his remuneration, but to a more remote feeling of being little better than a cog in the industrial machine. More misery is often caused by the bullying of a foreman or by precarious insecurity than by actual poverty. The improvement of the machine and the development of mass production methods have made labour *dull*. The growth of the big concern has removed the worker from any contact or consultation with those responsible for the direction of the business. He has ceased to be a skilled and valued craftsman and become a mere "hand", to be used or discarded by what must seem to him a hard and unrelenting mechanism with no interest in his welfare, and not requiring his interest in its own.

These disabilities must be overcome and removed, or compensated for in such a way as to render the worker's life more interesting and secure. The industrial system must be "humanised" in so far as the worker's position in it is concerned. The dullness of his labour must be compensated for by more leisure. But leisure is worthless unless it is accompanied by a tranquil state of mind and the opportunities for developing cultural life outside working hours. In Chapter V we saw that as a result of the system of regulation and order we have envisaged, the reduction of the hours of labour becomes "practical politics" for the first time. But there is also much to be done in the way of abolishing insecurity. The day to day or week to week engagement of labour is a vicious system, imposed upon us by the fluctuations of the market in an unregulated system. In the new system it would be possible to increase the proportion of permanent staff, introduce a new stability into working class life and break down the distinction between the black-coated and the manual workers by the institution of monthly, quarterly or yearly contracts. Similarly, the provision of holidays with pay and a continuation of wages during sickness, which is now granted without question to most salaried staffs, could be extended to the manual worker. These developments all become possible as a result of the greater *stability* we would have achieved by a conscious direction of policy.

It is not the purpose of this book to discuss alternative methods of supplementing the wages system, such as Profit-sharing or Co-partnership. But it should be noted that the difficulties of working such schemes in the past have mostly arisen from the instability of the market and the competitive conditions of "free Capitalism". In the new circumstance proposals of this kind might well be reviewed with the object of discovering a method by which the worker might be made to feel himself a real partner in the enterprise of the nation and of the industry in which he was engaged.

The tendency of the new system will be to reduce or eliminate speculative profits and, while leaving the principles of property and ownership, rule out the frenzied finance of the doubtful company promoter. It is this rather than the legitimate profit of the industrial shareholders which causes resentment, especially when slump follows boom and the worker is left to carry the burden of impoverishment and unemployment which follows. It is the profiteer who breeds the agitator.

Mere jealousy of people better off than themselves has never been an important element in the national character. What the British people want is a square deal, and to feel that they are being treated fairly. In a nation organised as has been suggested the accounts, costs and profits of the large integrated industries would be open and above-board. They would be scrutinised by other industries and subject to criticism as part of the task of maintaining equilibrium supervised by the Economic Council. As a result of this alone a great deal of the suspicion which is partly the cause of present unrest would be removed. The representation of the Trade Unions on the Economic Council and the regular consultation between management and labour throughout the whole parallel structure of organisation would provide a counterpart, in the economic sphere, to the political self-government which has been achieved through the extension of the franchise. The worker would no longer be treated as a commodity to be bought and sold in the labour market, but as an integral part of a united and coherent system.

The tendency, which Lord Milner foresaw more than twenty years ago, would be accentuated, towards a system in which management and labour would hire capital, rather than capital hiring management and labour. Usury and speculation, in the evil sense of the terms, would be eliminated, and the rewards of productive effort more equitably distributed. The status of labour in the industrial life of the community could be progressively changed by the co-operation of all classes in a common effort to construct a rational, intelligently managed system in which the welfare of every section of the community would be considered, not in relation to preconceived notions of rights or privileges, but in accordance with the wise direction of representative institutions basing their conclusions upon the facts.

A bridge might thus be built over the chasm of antagonisms which economic confusion and political passion have created, and all classes gradually led to a recognition of the simple fact that the prosperity of each part or section depends upon the prosperity of the nation as a whole.

CHAPTER IX

THE THREAT OF DICTATORSHIP: FASCISM AND COMMUNISM

THE policy which has been advocated in this book will no doubt be described as "Socialism" by some elements on the right, and as "Fascism" by some elements on the left. In fact these charges have already been made when the proposals were advanced in a much more tentative form in articles and speeches during the year 1932. The only importance of the use of these descriptions is that they are levelled as accusations calculated to arouse opposition by an appeal to prejudice. It is as well, therefore, that they should be categorically denied.

Fascism and Communism have some things in common. They both reject the idea of any form of representative and democratic government. They both hold that the conflicts of Capitalist society cannot be reconciled without resort to force—either for the coercion of "interests" or for the abolition of "interests." They believe that the only reality in the present situation is the struggle to capture State power. They have little belief in their ability to achieve power by constitutional means, and therefore they prepare to seize power by revolutionary action and civil war. Having seized power they would abolish political liberty in order to gain freedom from interruption in the task of establishing economic order. To maintain their power they would extirpate every opposing element whether the opposition was physical or merely intellectual. Freedom of speech would be abolished except for those who were content to repeat the formulas which had been approved for the time being by the group in authority. In the struggle to achieve power they would promote the "virile" elements among their followers to whom the positions of leadership in a movement of violence would naturally belong. They will boast that they are men of action—and indeed it will be true. The reflective intelligent elements who doubt whether economic problems can be solved with a bludgeon will be regarded as "weak" and "unreliable," and if these elements survive at all it will be as the docile and obedient slaves of the more "romantic" men of action.

And after all this play-acting and demagogy has had its run; when the intellectual and cultural expressions of every individual have been prostituted to the service of a vague mysticism called "the cause," beaten out of them with rubber truncheons or sweated out of them in concentration camps; when the school curriculum has been "cleaned up" and children taught to salute rather than to think; when all this has been done *they will be faced with precisely the same economic problems as those which confront us to-day.*

It is true that the degree of violence will depend to some extent on whether the leader with authority is a Mussolini or a Hitler; a Lenin or a Trotsky; but whoever he may be he will be faced with the necessity, if he adopts this course of action, of calling out those reckless elements in the struggle for power which he will find difficult to discard when power has been achieved. No doubt there are circumstances when men of intelligence who are also men of action could hardly be expected to resist the temptation to use the ignorant passion of the mob to assist them to achieve power. There may have been justification for the revolutionary movements which grew out of the chaotic conditions following upon the collapse of authority in Italy in 1922 and in Russia in 1917. But to suggest that we should deliberately seek a repetition of these conditions in Britain appeals neither to the reason nor the emotions of intelligent men.

Our task is to avoid collapse; to put forward our constructive suggestions now, and to offer co-operation and help to whatever set of leaders will adopt a policy adequate to the needs of our time. Fascism and Communism are movements of political revolution, which rest upon passion. The policy which has been advocated here is one of economic evolution which rests upon an appeal to reason.

However plausible and attractive the economics of Fascism and of Communism may be made to sound, it is the political part of their policy which must be borne in mind. The whole conception of political upheaval as a prelude to any action with regard to the practical bread-and-butter questions of the day is typical of the mentality of the political adventurer on the one hand or the dreamer of Utopias on the other. These mystical conceptions of the future of society are foreign to the practical mind of the ordinary adult British citizen. Their danger lies in the appeal to the romanticism of youth. They call for sacrifice, for a crusade, for devotion to some mystical ideal of a perfect society, and they would prostitute this idealism to the horrible purposes of violence and of war. There is a latent nobility also in the more brutal types of individuals. These movements of violence appeal to that, and provide the pervert with the opportunity of exercising his brutality under the cloak of justification provided by his "good intentions."

Movements of this kind cannot be frustrated by a merely negative attitude. Nor can they be thwarted by the vilification of their leaders, for the leaders are often sincere, inasmuch as they deceive themselves as well as their followers. We must challenge them with a positive alternative. Our policy must be adequate and comprehensive. It must satisfy the impatience which has been engendered by years of futility and delay. We must prove in action that the problems confronting us are capable of solution without bloodshed and violence, or the sacrifice of those liberties to which we have become so accustomed as hardly to remember their value.

In the proposals which have been elaborated in this book there will be found, it is true, points of similarity with the structure of organisation in the Russian Communist State and the Italian Corporate State. These points of similarity will occur in all economic systems where planning and conscious direction take the place of the confusion of the free market. But the idea of planning is neither Fascist nor Communist. The idea of the Corporate State was an afterthought of the Italian revolution. The Russian Five-Year Plan was formulated ten years after the Bolsheviks came to power. The revolutionary movements existed before their economic policies were even conceived. Advocates of economic planning must be careful, therefore, to make it clear that the economic policy they preach is never confused with the political doctrines of those who are willing to preach any policy likely to win for them the power for which they crave to the point of obsession.

The organisational structure described in this book provides for the creation of what may be called Monopolies or Trusts. There are Trusts in Russia and Industrial Corporations with monopoly powers in Italy; but that does not make the proposals here advanced either Communist or Fascist. The political theory of Dictatorship is here rejected in favour of a structure of industrial self-government.

Such a structure seems to us more in the true tradition of English development than either of these exotic cults. While individualism and *laissez-faire* distinguished too rigidly between man as a producer and man as a citizen, do not let us rush wildly to the other extreme. Discipline and efficiency can be accepted in their limited application to the economic processes of society without any corresponding regulation of the human spirit in its widest sense. And while we recognise that the growth of individualism tended to obscure that organic conception of society which was the distinct contribution of mediæval thought, yet we need not be pushed into an exaggeration of this doctrine. Society is entitled to demand that each individual should co-operate in the organised effort to perform efficiently the material tasks of production on which the mutual welfare of citizens depend. But the object of this economic efficiency must be to enhance for the individual citizen his opportunities of political, intellectual and cultural freedom. There is no necessity to surrender these individual rights in order to find a solution of the economic problems confronting us. Parliament has already all the influence and power it requires to lead the nation out of the depression, which attends the decline of the old system, into the prosperity which would follow from the adjustments of our economic life in accordance with the facts of the modern world. A Government which gave this lead to the nation would relieve us for all time from the dangers of Dictatorships and the catastrophe of violence. There is need for a mobilisation of all the moderate and intelligent elements in the country who are not misled by temporary indications of recovery into believing that everything will come right of its own accord. These elements are sufficiently numerous and influential to ensure that the drastic changes which are seen to be essential when the real nature of the crisis is understood, are carried out with courage and with expedition. The flamboyant appeal of the revolutionary must be opposed not by a negative attitude, but by constructive proposals which appeal to the reason and intelligence of the nation, and which can be shown both in argument and in practice to be adequate for the creation of a system in which we shall be able to enjoy the fruits of increased productivity made possible by the bounty of Nature and the applied genius of Mankind. It may be an additional attraction to some minds at least, if such a system is able to provide a reasonable compromise between the rival claims of individualist and collectivist conceptions of society—a compromise which might enable the nobler aspects of each to be retained.

It would be not the least of the many contributions of the English genius to human progress if, in the midst of the hysteria which has attacked the world, we were to produce a new synthesis of these two currents of political thought. It would be in keeping with our tradition and in harmony with the desire of a nation long skilled in the art of government.

APPENDIX

SUMMARIES

IMPORTS (Value C.I.F.*)

	Year ended 31st December.		
	1930.	1931.	1932.
I.—*Food, Drink and Tobacco*—	£	£	£
A. Grain and Flour	72,803,831	55,818,037	58,045,656
B. Feeding-stuffs for Animals	5,745,034	5,379,631	6,540,249
C. Meat	111,526,075	93,905,248	81,385,317
D. Animals, Living, for Food	18,317,811	16,014,663	10,657,296
E and F. Other Food and Drink	251,003,510	234,227,624	207,896,186
G. Tobacco	15,719,822	11,376,456	10,154,920
Total, Class I.	475,116,083	416,721,659	374,679,624
II.—*Raw Materials and Articles Mainly Unmanufactured*—			
A. Coal	29,120	34,381	26,609
B. Other Non-Metallic Mining and Quarry Products and the like	5,268,317	3,919,570	3,450,203
C. Iron Ore and Scrap	5,161,302	2,336,590	1,891,701
D. Non-Ferrous Metalliferous Ores and Scrap	12,231,998	7,229,515	6,093,257
E. Wood and Timber	42,774,541	29,140,529	25,601,990
F. Raw Cotton and Cotton Waste	44,989,749	27,182,530	31,111,187
G. Wool, Raw and Waste, and Woollen Rags	45,102,389	34,544,409	33,577,548
H. Silk, Raw, Knubs and Noils	1,515,363	1,238,714	1,374,033
I. Other Textile Materials	9,584,083	7,035,974	6,745,727
J. Oil Seeds, Nuts, Oils, Fats, Resins and Gums	33,658,484	24,964,275	22,569,853
K. Hides and Skins, Undressed	16,126,020	11,696,212	12,100,649
L. Paper-making Materials	12,073,971	9,976,964	9,801,535
M. Rubber	10,722,498	4,496,458	2,466,692
N. Miscellaneous Raw Materials and Articles mainly Unmanufactured	11,220,980	9,242,089	7,650,782
Total, Class II.	250,458,815	173,038,210	164,461,766
III.—*Articles Wholly or Mainly Manufactured*—			
A. Coke and Manufactured Fuel	10,000	18,181	24,458
B. Pottery, Glass, Abrasives, etc.	10,900,454	9,603,200	5,130,942
C. Iron and Steel and Manufactures thereof	23,298,894	19,621,620	8,665,241
D. Non-Ferrous Metals and Manufactures thereof	29,362,996	21,408,132	14,702,240
E. Cutlery, Hardware, Implements and Instruments	7,702,204	7,275,917	4,508,825
F. Electrical Goods and Apparatus	7,026,676	6,239,770	2,736,492
G. Machinery	17,920,478	15,339,031	10,329,691
H. Manufactures of Wood and Timber	8,738,641	7,533,142	5,445,723
I. Cotton Yarns and Manufactures	9,735,503	8,942,242	1,891,777
J. Woollen and Worsted Yarns and Manufactures.	14,266,774	13,446,767	2,363,180
K. Silk Yarns and Manufactures	11,220,901	8,392,892	3,807,832
L. Manufactures of other Textile Materials	15,334,860	14,942,794	8,747,486
M. Apparel	19,290,632	19,838,807	7,027,404
N. Chemicals, Drugs, Dyes and Colours	13,571,388	13,841,670	9,578,482
O. Oils, Fats and Resins, Manufactured	46,241,999	29,415,121	31,050,129
P. Leather and Manufactures thereof	15,255,874	13,239,940	7,674,170
Q. Paper and Cardboard	17,975,372	16,431,232	13,088,790
R. Vehicles (including Locomotives, Ships and Aircraft)	6,827,794	4,240,095	3,119,176
S. Rubber Manufactures	3,927,290	3,429,850	1,786,257
T. Miscellaneous Articles wholly or mainly Manufactured	28,809,145	28,518,032	15,997,363
Total, Class III.	307,417,875	261,718,435	157,675,658
IV.—*Animals, not for Food*	3,679,927	3,329,000	2,188,686
V.—*Parcel Post*	7,302,561	6,445,334	4,126,991
TOTAL	**1,043,975,261**	**861,252,638**	**703,132,725**

* The value of the imports represents the cost, insurance, and freight; or, when goods are consigned for sale, the latest sale value of such goods.

NAVIGATION ACCOUNTS

SUMMARIES

EXPORTS OF PRODUCE AND MANUFACTURES OF THE UNITED KINGDOM (Value F.O.B.*)

	Year ended 31st December.		
	1930.	1931.	1932.
I.—*Food, Drink and Tobacco*—	£	£	£
A. Grain and Flour	4,256,047	3,316,315	3,315,609
B. Feeding-stuffs for Animals	2,171,957	2,087,174	1,578,221
C. Meat	1,487,813	1,230,511	1,060,028
D. Animals, Living, for Food	221,633	171,989	93,704
E and F. Other Food and Drink	31,598,429	23,499,986	22,080,872
G. Tobacco	8,482,673	5,216,377	4,199,877
Total, Class I.	48,218,552	35,522,352	32,328,311
II.—*Raw Materials and Articles Mainly Unmanufactured*—			
A. Coal	45,661,280	34,653,774	31,634,043
B. Other Non-Metallic Mining and Quarry Products and the like	1,649,781	1,082,616	870,967
C. Iron Ore and Scrap	568,200	420,904	259,906
D. Non-Ferrous Metalliferous Ores and Scrap	751,402	457,843	741,098
E. Wood and Timber	281,015	230,024	117,056
F. Raw Cotton and Cotton Waste	600,209	331,547	495,430
G. Wool, Raw and Waste, and Woollen Rags	4,810,931	3,270,996	3,453,964
H. Silk, Raw, Knubs and Noils	14,195	11,963	9,885
I. Other Textile Materials	267,770	201,335	356,365
J. Oil Seeds, Nuts, Oils, Fats, Resins and Gums	3,618,620	2,438,216	1,852,199
K. Hides and Skins, Undressed	1,438,042	742,176	514,530
L. Paper-making Materials	1,048,109	684,006	755,567
M. Rubber	174,600	104,920	113,464
N. Miscellaneous Raw Materials and Articles mainly Unmanufactured	2,876,344	2,409,076	2,451,193
Total, Class II.	63,760,498	47,039,396	43,625,667
III.—*Articles Wholly or Mainly Manufactured*—			
A. Coke and Manufactured Fuel	3,547,800	2,960,349	2,641,635
B. Pottery, Glass, Abrasives, etc.	11,900,652	8,407,468	7,419,913
C. Iron and Steel and Manufactures thereof	51,261,119	30,375,155	28,044,950
D. Non-Ferrous Metals and Manufactures thereof	12,037,798	6,941,361	6,891,584
E. Cutlery, Hardware, Implements and Instruments	7,336,254	5,333,526	5,554,953
F. Electrical Goods and Apparatus	11,927,934	7,437,944	5,848,370
G. Machinery	46,974,006	33,011,639	29,528,768
H. Manufactures of Wood and Timber	2,215,409	1,426,965	1,193,022
I. Cotton Yarns and Manufactures	87,586,591	56,598,134	62,845,351
J. Woollen and Worsted Yarns and Manufactures.	36,962,726	25,150,313	24,004,111
K. Silk Yarns and Manufactures	1,555,564	1,037,560	1,023,867
L. Manufactures of other Textile Materials	19,557,521	12,884,985	13,151,958
M. Apparel	19,768,021	14,014,095	11,829,755
N. Chemicals, Drugs, Dyes and Colours	21,958,476	17,017,839	17,377,524
O. Oils, Fats and Resins, Manufactured	7,459,809	5,305,754	5,158,844
P. Leather and Manufactures thereof	5,261,906	3,313,955	2,965,186
Q. Paper and Cardboard	8,468,315	6,324,269	6,509,193
R. Vehicles (including Locomotives, Ships and Aircraft)	50,992,306	29,713,371	20,743,746†
S. Rubber Manufactures	2,829,532	2,137,182	1,942,966
T. Miscellaneous Articles wholly or mainly Manufactured	30,440,040	22,636,715	20,925,992
Total, Class III.	440,041,779	292,028,579	275,601,688†
IV.—*Animals, not for Food*	1,502,029	1,094,274	618,387
V.—*Parcel Post*	17,232,558	14,936,997	12,963,732
TOTAL	**570,755,416**	**390,621,598**	**365,137,785†**

* The value of the exports represents the cost and the charges of delivering the goods on board the ship, and is known as the "free on board" value.

† Amended aggregates.

PRINTED IN GREAT BRITAIN BY
RICHARD CLAY & SONS, LIMITED,
BUNGAY, SUFFOLK.